A PHOTO

SNAKES

AND OTHER REPTILES OF

BORNEO

INDRANEIL DAS

Originally published in 2006 by New Holland Publishers (UK) Ltd.
London • Cape Town • Sydney • Auckland
www.newhollandpublishers.com

Garfield House, 86–88 Edgware Road, London W2 2EA, United Kingdom
80 McKenzie Street, Cape Town 8001, South Africa
Unit 1, 66 Gibbes Street, Chatswood, New South Wales, Australia 2067
218 Lake Road, Northcote, Auckland, New Zealand

Second edition 2011

ISBN: 978 1 84773 881 3

Senior Editor: Krystyna Mayer (2011 edition)

Project Editor: Gareth Jones
Editor: Robert Watts
Designer: Gülen Shevki-Taylor
Cartographer: William Smuts
Production: Joan Woodroffe

Reproduction by Modern Age Repro House Limited, Hong Kong
Printed and bound in Malaysia by Times Offset (M) Sdn Bhd

10 9 8 7 6 5 4 3 2 1

Acknowledgements
I thank the Sarawak Forest Department, the Sarawak Forestry Corporation, Sabah Parks and the Brunei Forestry Department, for permits and facilities to work in areas under their jurisdiction.
My research on the herpetofauna of Borneo has been supported by the Institute of Biodiversity and Environmental Conservation, Universiti Malaysia Sarawak (UNIMAS), through grants (120(98) 9, 192(99) 46, 1/26/303/2002 (40), 01/59/376/2003 (113) and 01/94/441/2004 (179), as well as an Intensification of Research in Priority Areas (IRPA) Grant from Ministry of Higher Education, Malaysia (08-02-09-10007-EA0001), and Universiti Brunei Darussalam, through its research fellowship programme. I am grateful to a large number of colleagues at these institutions, including Andrew Alek Tuen, Ghazally Ismail, Stuart James Davies, Nicolas Pilcher, Joseph Kirbahkaran Charles, David Sydney Edwards, David Thomas Jones, Helen Pang, Samhan bin Nyawa and Kamariah Abu Salim, for support and encouragement of my field and laboratory investigations. For use of photographs, I am grateful to Mark Auliya, Alain Compost, John G. Frazier, Robert Frederick Inger, Tan Heok Hui, Björn Lardner, Norman Lim, Aaron Lobo, Ulrich Manthey, Showichi Sengoku, Jeet Sukumaran Gernot Vogel and Robert Voeks. I'd like to thank a number of colleagues, Kraig Adler, Christopher Austin, Aaron Bauer, Ronald Crombie, Patrick David, David Gower, Allen Greer, Tsutomu Hikida, Marinus Hoogmoed, Ivan Ineich, Robert F. Inger, Djoko Iskandar, Lim Chan Koon, Kelvin K. P. Lim, Colin J. McCarthy, Ulrich Manthey, Peter K.L. Ng, Hidetoshi Ota, José Rosado, Robert Stuebing, Tan Heok Hui, Jens Vindum, Harold Voris, Van Wallach and George R. Zug, for making available publications, aiding fieldwork, or generally providing support for the preparation of this work. Finally, I am grateful to my wife, Genevieve V.A. Gee, for reading and commenting on a draft of the book. I dedicate this book to the new addition to our family, Rahul, born when it was being written.

Contents

Introduction

The island of Borneo stretches between co-ordinates 04°S–07°N and from 109–119°E and sits on the Sundas Shelf. It is the second largest tropical island in the world (after New Guinea), and covers a land area of approximately 743,380km². A major part of Borneo (539,460km²) lies within Kalimantan, which belongs to the Republic of Indonesia. Other political units within the island are the east Malaysian states of Sarawak (124,450km²), Sabah (73,710km²) and the Sultanate of Brunei Darussalam (5,760km²).

At 4,101m, Low's Peak in Gunung Kinabalu, northern Sabah, is the highest peak on Borneo. The summit of Kinabalu shows evidence of glaciation, including polished and grooved rock surfaces. The highest mountain in Sarawak, at 2,423m, is Gunung Murud. The Subis limestone complex of Niah, Sarawak, was home to early hominids, about 40,000 years before present. A spectacular limestone formation, including extensive cave systems, is to be found in the Gunung Mulu region of Sarawak.

Several of the largest rivers of south-east Asia flow through Borneo. Important rivers of the Sarawak region – which all drain into the South China Sea – include the Baram and the Lupar. Significant rivers of Sabah include the Segama and the Kinabatangan. Kalimantan's great rivers include the Kapuas, Barito, Kahayan, Kayan and Mahakam. Many of the coastal rivers are broad and meandering.

Borneo lies within the tropics and the equator crosses this great island approximately over Pontianak in Kalimantan. The island is

characterized by relatively high, equitable temperature and heavy rainfall, which is spread virtually throughout the year. The relatively wetter periods are observed during the passage of the north-east monsoons (November–April), although the south-west monsoons (April–August) also bring rainfall to the area. Daytime temperatures in most parts of the low-lying areas are 30–32°C, and humidity is typically high. Annual precipitation is in the range 4,000–5,000mm. A major influence of short-term climatic fluctuations in Borneo and across the Indo-Pacific region is the El Niño, which brings uncontrolled forest fires, leading to haze, water shortage and loss of crops, land and life. The advent of the north-east monsoons between December–February brings much precipitation to the area.

Vegetation

The plant life of Borneo is characterized by high species diversity and low endemism, the latter attributed to the land connection during the lowered sea-levels of the Pleistocene. For instance, the Kinabalu flora itself comprises as many as 5,000–6,000 species, including over 1,000 genera and 200 families. The richest forests of south-east Asia are in north-western Borneo, north of Sungei Kapuas in the west, encompassing the north-east portion of Sarawak, Brunei and the south-western lowlands of Sabah. The region is, in geological terms, relatively young, has a rugged topography, comprising mostly infertile shallow soils, compared to other areas of Borneo.

Vegetational zonation here is best known from Gunung Kinabalu. The lowland forest is six-layered, with emergent trees and sparse undergrowth. The upper boundary of lowland rainforest is at about 1,200m, where the majority of emergent trees – comprising primarily the dipterocarps – disappear from the canopy. The lower montane forest is five-layered, lacking emergents. The upper limit of the lower montane forest is 2,000–2,350m; that of the upper montane forest, between 2,800–3,000m. The upper montane forest has a dense herbaceous layer. The upper limit of the lower subalpine coniferous forests is 3,400m, which is sparse in undergrowth and lower in height. Fragmented upper subalpine forests occur at an altitude of 3,700m. Above this is a zone of alpine rock-desert, with scattered communities of alpine scrub.

Important forest types include mixed dipterocarp forest from the yellow-red soils in the uplands, dominated by *Dryobalanops lanceolata*, *Shorea parviflora*, *Dryobalanops aromatica* and *Dipterocarpus globosus*. The lower montane and upper montane forests are also remarkable in their structure and composition. Canopy height is reduced, sometimes to 18–30m, with few emergent trees; buttressed trees are less common, and there is an absence of large woody climbers, but a great abundance of vascular epiphytes. Moss vegetation, with an abundance of bryophytes, in addition to gnarled trees, characterise the upper limits of montane forests. Upper montane forests also have trees with small, leathery leaves and conifers.

Another distinctive vegetation type is the heath forests or Kerangas, confined to either raised beach terraces or sandstone ridges and plateaux, represented by the families Myrtaceae, Theaceae and Podocarpaceae. Peat swamp forest is another vegetation type, especially extensive along the north-western coast of Borneo. They lie within present or former areas of swamp forests, and are either slow-flowing or nearly stagnant. Plant species diversity is low, with only 317 species recorded, and few endemics. A distinctive vegetation type is limestone flora, which is rich in plant and invertebrate (especially molluscan) endemics. Mangrove forests, which are rich in species, especially at the mouth of Sungei Kinabatangan and in Brunei Bay, is yet another noteworthy vegetation type.

Biodiversity and conservation

Despite the long history of explorations, the biodiversity of Borneo has been only partially documented. As many as 11,000 species of flowering plants, about a third of which are endemic, have been recorded. Here, a 16 acre forest may have over 700 species of trees, as opposed to only 50 in northern Europe or 171 in eastern North America. Endemicity is high in the plant life of Borneo. Among the dipterocarps, 267 species have been recorded on Borneo, 155 of which are endemic.

Rates of deforestation are alarmingly high throughout much of Borneo. Nonetheless, protected area systems exist throughout the island, some of which have geographic continuity. Primary reasons for forest loss include logging for timber, clearing of land for agriculture, urbanisation and settlement. In Kalimantan, a major transmigration programme was conducted to settle people from the densely populated Indonesian islands. During the dry season, many forest types are prone to fire, accidentally started, or used by settlers to clear vegetation to prepare the land for agriculture, including oil palm plantations. Vast tracts of what were once unbroken primary forests have been lost to forest fires in the last decade, also causing atmospheric pollution, and loss of human lives. Other factors responsible for degradation of forest land within Borneo include swidden cultivation, removal of minor forest produce, and conversion of forest habitats to grasslands.

Snakebite and management

Borneo is home to a several species of venomous snakes. However, most of these are found far from human settlements, a situation unlike that seen in many other tropical regions, where snakes are common in rural areas, plantations and agricultural fields, due to the abundance of rats. As a result, the number of deaths from snakebite on the island is negligible. Nonetheless, I provide here some precautionary measures for those who deal with venomous reptiles in a professional capacity, are interested in their natural history, or simply encounter them while in the field.

Because there are only a few deadly venomous snakes, it is useful to be able to identify them. **Vipers** are relatively slow-moving snakes, with narrow necks and broad heads. Their fangs are folded back when not in use. **Cobras** are large, heavy-bodied snakes that may erect their bodies and spread their hood by erecting the ribs in the neck. They have short, fixed fangs. **Coral snakes** and **kraits** belong to the same family, but cannot spread a hood. **Sea snakes** are large and slender-bodied, with flat tails, and are nearly always marine, or at least coastal, in distribution, although some might travel a considerable distance upriver. The **sea kraits** come on land, and can, in fact, even climb trees. They have short, fixed fangs.

A word of caution: several non-venomous snakes mimic dangerous snakes, and the reverse can also be true! Many snakes (such as the **cat snakes** and some of the **keelbacks**) that do not bear true venom glands can nonetheless inflict painful bites, sometimes aided by a chewing motion, that could lead to complications.

When in the field, avoid putting your hand inside cracks or holes which might conceal a snake. Wear shoes that completely conceal the feet in the forest, and always carry a reliable torch. Headlamps, such as the type used by miners (although lighter ones are now produced by camping goods companies), are even better, as they keep both hands free. When crossing a fallen tree, look carefully underneath it on both sides (particularly the blind side). Keep houses and their surroundings free of garbage and litter, as these attract rats, which, in turn, attract snakes.

Permits are required for collecting and keeping reptiles, for scientific purposes. When handling a snake for study or photography, use a restrainer, such as a snake hook (typically an L-shaped stick) or better still, a snake tong. Store live snakes (and other reptiles) in cloth bags; check for holes and other weaknesses along the seams. If you are keeping snakes live in aquaria/terraria, ensure that the lid is secure. Landscape the enclosure with plenty of places for concealment (such as bits of bark and vegetation, as well as rocks) and provide drinking water for reptiles that are otherwise being kept dry. Avoid keeping venomous or unknown snakes: remember that they not only pose a hazard to you, but also to your family and neighbours.

The anti-venom serum commonly available locally is imported from Australia, India and Thailand, and is available in most hospitals and primary health centres. As most bites occur in forested or coastal areas, the patient should be reassured and kept warm, have the region of their bite immobilized using a crepe (or any other stiff cloth) bandage, and be brought to the hospital as quickly as possible (being carried there, if needs be). In case of breathing difficulties, such as those shown after envenoming by cobras and kraits, the patient may require artificial respiration. It helps the treatment of the patient if an accurate description of the snake can be provided. Do not apply a tourniquet, cut or suck the wound, or give aspirin, as these are likely to complicate the treatment as well as the subsequent healing process. In the unlikely event of a snakebite, remember that no snake can kill a healthy adult human being instantaneously, and if treated appropriately, most patients make a complete recovery.

About this book

At present, 293 species (160 snakes, 111 lizards, 19 turtles and tortoises and three crocodiles) have been recorded from the island of Borneo. This photographic guide describes and illustrates 187 of these (90 snakes, 80 lizards, 15 turtles and two crocodiles), including the more abundant and many otherwise distinctive species of snakes, lizards, crocodiles and turtles that one is likely to encounter, representing many genera. Not included in the work are two exotic (ie, non-native) species – the Red-eared Slider (*Trachemys scripta*) and Chinese Softshell Turtle (*Pelodiscus sinensis*) – that are now introduced into waterbodies in the island through the pet or food trade. For every species covered, there is a brief description (scale counts and other data) and a summary of available information on the biology of the species, in addition to one or more colour photographs.

Each species account comprises a recommended English name, the current scientific name, a brief description and a summary of its biology and distribution within Borneo and elsewhere. Length given is the maximum recorded for individual species – snout-vent length for snakes, lizards and crocodiles, and straight carapace length for turtles and tortoises. All measurements are in mm, except for species that attain maximum sizes of 100cm plus. Listing of species is by groups (snakes, followed by lizards, crocodiles and turtles), and within these, by families, genera and species, in alphabetical order. Finding species is thus by locating the picture that matches a particular species, and confirming from the morphological description and colouration, as well as distribution and biology, provided in the text. A word of caution: this work does not pretend to be comprehensive, and therefore, specialist readers may wish to confirm identification with more technical works on the subject (listed towards the end of book). The Bornean herpetofauna is not completely known, and many species remains to be recognised by science. Several other species are in the process of being described, either by me or by colleagues, one (a skink) of which has been covered in this book, without applying a scientific name, which will be done in the technical literature.

A checklist of the reptiles of Borneo. Introduced species indicated with an asterisk.

ACROCHORDIDAE
Acrochordus granulatus
(Schneider, 1799)
Acrochordus javanicus
Hornstedt, 1787

ANOMOCHILIDAE
Anomochilus leonardi
Smith, 1940
Anomochilus weberi
(van Lidth de Jeude, 1890)
Anomochilus monticola

PYTHONIDAE
Broghammerus reticulatus
(Schneider, 1801)
Python breitensteini
Steindachner, 1881

COLUBRIDAE
Ahaetulla fasciolata
(Fischer, 1885)
Ahaetulla prasina
(Boie, 1827)

Amphiesma flavifrons (Boulenger, 1887)
Amphiesma frenata (Dunn, 1923)
Amphiesma petersi (Boulenger, 1893)
Amphiesma sarawacense (Günther, 1872)
Aplopeltura boa Boie, 1828
Asthenodipsas laevis (Boie, 1827)
Asthenodipsas malaccanus Peters, 1864
Asthenodipsas vertebralis (Boulenger, 1900)
Boiga cynodon (H. Boie in F. Boie, 1827)
Boiga dendrophila (Boie, 1827)
Boiga drapiezii (H. Boie in F. Boie, 1827)
Boiga jaspidea Duméril, Bibron & Duméril, 1854
Boiga nigriceps (Günther, 1863)
Calamaria battersbyi Marx & Inger, 1965
Calamaria bicolor Duméril, Bibron & Duméril, 1854
Calamaria borneensis Bleeker, 1860
Calamaria everetti Boulenger, 1893
Calamaria grabowskyi Fischer, 1885
Calamaria gracillima (Günther, 1872)
Calamaria griswoldi Loveridge, 1938
Calamaria hillenuisi Inger & Marx, 1965
Calamaria lateralis Mocquard, 1890
Calamaria leucogaster Bleeker, 1860
Calamaria lovii Boulenger, 1887
Calamaria lumbricoidea H. Boie in: F. Boie, 1827
Calamaria lumholtzi Andersson, 1923
Calamaria melanota Jan, 1862
Calamaria modesta Duméril, Bibron & Duméril, 1854
Calamaria prakkei van Lidth de Jeude, 1893
Calamaria rebentischi Bleeker, 1860
Calamaria schlegeli Duméril, Bibron & Duméril, 1854
Calamaria schmidti Marx & Inger, 1955
Calamaria suluensis Taylor, 1922
Calamaria virgulata H. Boie in: F. Boie, 1827
Cantoria violacea Girard, 1857
Cerberus rynchops (Schneider, 1799)
Chrysopelea paradisi H. Boie in F. Boie, 1827
Chrysopelea pelias (Linnaeus, 1758)
Coelognathus erythrurus (Duméril, Bibron & Duméril, 1854)
Coelognathus flavolineatus (Schlegel, 1837)
Coelognathus radiatus (Boie, 1827)
Dendrelaphis caudolineatus (Gray, 1834)
Dendrelaphis formosus Boie, 1827
Dendrelaphis kopsteini Vogel & van Rooijen (2007)
Dendrelaphis pictus (Gmelin, 1789)
Dendrelaphis striatus (Cohn, 1905)
Dryocalamus subannulatus Duméril, Bibron, Duméril, 1854
Dryocalamus tristrigatus Günther, 1858
Dryophiops rubescens (Gray, 1834)
Elapoidis fuscus Boie, 1827
Enhydris alternans (Reuss, 1834)
Enhydris doriae (Peters, 1871)
Enhydris enhydris (Schneider, 1799)
Enhydris plumbea (H. Boie in F. Boie, 1827)
Enhydris punctata (Gray, 1849)
Fordonia leucobalia (Schlegel, 1837)
Gongylosoma balodeirum (Boie, 1827)
Gongylosoma longicauda (Peters, 1871)
Gonyophis margaritatus (Peters, 1871)
Gonyosoma oxycephalum (Boie, 1827)
Homalopsis buccata (Linnaeus, 1758)
Hydrablabes periops (Günther, 1872)

Hydrablabes praefrontalis (Mocquard, 1890)
Lepturophis borneensis Boulenger, 1900
Liopeltis tricolor (Schlegel, 1837)
Lycodon albofuscus (Duméril, Bibron & Duméril, 1854)
Lycodon capucinus Boie, 1827
Lycodon effraenis Cantor, 1847
Lycodon subcinctus Boie, 1827
Macropisthodon flaviceps (Duméril, Bibron & Duméril, 1854)
Macropisthodon rhodomelas (H. Boie in F. Boie, 1827)
Oligodon annulifer (Boulenger, 1893)
Oligodon cinereus (Günther, 1864)
Oligodon everetti Boulenger, 1893
Oligodon octolineatus (Schneider, 1801)
Oligodon purpurascens (Schlegel, 1837)
Oligodon semicinctus (Peters, 1862)
Oligodon signatus (Günther, 1872)
Oligodon vertebralis (Günther, 1865)
Opisthotropis typica (Mocquard, 1890)
Oreocalamus hanitschi Boulenger, 1899
Orthriophis taeniurus (Cope, 1861)
Pareas carinatus (Boie, 1828)
Pareas nuchalis (Boulenger, 1900)
Psammodynastes pictus (Günther, 1858)
Psammodynastes pulverulentus (H. Boie in F. Boie, 1827)
Pseudorabdion albonuchalis (Günther, 1896)
Pseudorabdion collaris (Mocquard, 1892)
Pseudorabdion longiceps (Cantor, 1847)
Pseudorabdion saravacensis (Shelford, 1901)
Pseudoxenodon baramensis (Smith, 1921)
Ptyas carinata (Günther, 1858)
Ptyas fusca (Günther, 1858)
Ptyas korros (Schlegel, 1837)
Rhabdophis chrysargos (Schlegel, 1837)
Rhabdophis conspicillatus (Günther, 1872)
Rhabdophis murudensis (Smith, 1925)
Rhabdophis subminiatus (Schlegel, 1837)
Sibynophis geminatus (Boie, 1826)
Sibynophis melanocephalus (Gray, 1834)
Stegonotus borneensis Inger, 1967
Stoliczkia borneensis Boulenger, 1899
Xenelaphis ellipsifer Boulenger, 1900
Xenelaphis hexagonotus (Cantor, 1847)
Xenochrophis maculatus (Edeling, 1865)
Xenochrophis trianguligerus (Boie, 1827)
Xenodermus javanicus Reinhardt, 1836

CYLINDROPHIIDAE

Cylindrophis engkariensis Stuebing, 1994
Cylindrophis lineatus Blanford, 1881
Cylindrophis ruffus (Laurenti, 1768)

ELAPIDAE

Bungarus fasciatus (Schneider, 1801)
Bungarus flaviceps Reinhardt, 1843
Calliophis bivirgata (Boie, 1827)
Calliophis intestinalis (Laurenti, 1768)
Naja sumatrana Müller, 1887
Ophiophagus hannah (Cantor, 1836)

HYDROPHIIDAE

Aipysurus eydouxii (Gray, 1849)
Enhydrina schistosa (Daudin, 1803)
Hydrophis aagaardi Smith, 1920
Hydrophis brookii Günther, 1872

Hydrophis caerulescens (Shaw, 1802)
Hydrophis cyanocinctus Daudin, 1803
Hydrophis fasciatus (Schneider, 1799)
Hydrophis gracilis (Shaw, 1802)
Hydrophis klossi Boulenger, 1912
Hydrophis melanosoma Günther, 1864
Hydrophis ornatus (Gray, 1842)
Hydrophis sibauensis Rasmussen, Auliya & Böhme, 2001
Hydrophis spiralis (Shaw, 1802)
Kerilia jerdoni Gray, 1849
Kolpophis annandalei Laidlaw, 1901
Lapemis curtus Shaw, 1802
Laticauda colubrina (Schneider, 1799)
Laticauda laticaudata (Linnaeus, 1758)
Pelamis platura (Linnaeus, 1766)
Praescutata viperina (Schmidt, 1852)
Thalassophis anomalus (Schmidt, 1852)

TYPHLOPIDAE

Ramphotyphlops braminus (Daudin, 1803)
Ramphotyphlops lineatus (Schlegel, 1839)
Ramphotyphlops lorenzi (Werner, 1909)
Ramphotyphlops olivaceus (Gray, 1845)
Typhlops koekkoeki Brongersma, 1934
Typhlops muelleri Schlegel, 1839

VIPERIDAE

Garthius chaseni (Smith, 1931)
Popeia sabahi (Regenass & Kramer, 1981)
Parias sumatranus (Raffles, 1822)
Trimeresurus borneensis Peters, 1871
Trimeresurus malcolmi Loveridge, 1938
Tropidolaemus subannulatus (Gray, 1842)

XENOPELTIDAE

Xenopeltis unicolor (Boie, 1827)

XENOPHIDIIDAE

Xenophidion acanthognathus Günther & Manthey, 1995

AGAMIDAE

Aphaniotis acutirostris Modigliani, 1889
Aphaniotis fusca (Peters, 1864)
Aphaniotis ornata (van Lidth de Jeude, 1893)
Bronchocela cristatella (Kuhl, 1820)
Bronchocela jubata Duméril & Bibron, 1837
Complicitus nigrigularis (Ota & Hikida, 1991)
Draco cornutus Günther, 1864
Draco cristatellus Günther, 1872
Draco fimbriatus Kuhl, 1820
Draco haematopogon Boie in: Gray, 1831
Draco maximus Boulenger, 1893
Draco melanopogon Boulenger, 1887
Draco obscurus Boulenger, 1887
Draco quinquefasciatus Hardwicke & Gray, 1827
Draco sumatranus Schlegel, 1844
Gonocephalus bornensis (Schlegel, 1848)
Gonocephalus doriae (Peters, 1871)
Gonocephalus grandis (Gray, 1845)
Gonocephalus liogaster (Günther, 1872)
Gonocephalus mjobergi Smith, 1925
Harpesaurus borneensis (Mertens, 1924)
Hypsicalotes kinabaluensis (De Grijs, 1937)
Phoxophrys borneensis Inger, 1960
Phoxophrys cephalum (Mocquard, 1890)
Phoxophrys nigrilabris (Peters, 1864)
Phoxophrys spiniceps Smith, 1925

Pseudocalotes sarawacensis Inger & Stuebing, 1994

ANGUIDAE

Ophisaurus buettikoferi van Lidth de Jeude, 1905

EUBLEPHARIDAE

Aeluroscalabotes felinus (Günther, 1864)

DIBAMIDAE

Dibamus ingeri Das & Lim, 2003
Dibamus leucurus (Bleeker,1860)
Dibamus vorisi Das & Lim, 2003

GEKKONIDAE

Cnemaspis dringi Das & Bauer, 1998
Cnemaspis kendallii (Gray, 1845)
Cnemaspis nigridia (Smith, 1925)
Cnemaspis paripari Grismer & Chan, 2009
Cyrtodactylus baluensis (Mocquard, 1890)
Cyrtodactylus cavernicolus Inger & King, 1961
Cyrtodactylus consobrinus (Peters, 1871)
Cyrtodactylus ingeri Hikida, 1990
Cyrtodactylus malayanus (De Rooij, 1915)
Cyrtodactylus matsuii Hikida, 1990
Cyrtodactylus pubisulcus Inger, 1957
Cyrtodactylus quadrivirgatus Taylor, 1962
Cyrtodactylus yoshii Hikida, 1990
Gehyra mutilata (Wiegmann, 1834)
Gekko gecko Linnaeus, 1758
Gekko monarchus (Duméril & Bibron, 1836)
Gekko smithii (Gray, 1842)
Hemidactylus brookii Gray, 1845
Hemidactylus craspedotus (Mocquard, 1890)
Hemidactylus frenatus Duméril & Bibron, 1836
Hemidactylus garnotii Duméril & Bibron, 1836
Hemidactylus platyurus (Schneider, 1792)
Hemiphyllodactylus typus Bleeker, 1860
Lepidodactylus lugubris (Duméril & Bibron, 1836)
Lepidodactylus ranauensis Ota & Hikida, 1988
Luperosaurus browni Russell, 1979
Luperosaurus sorok Das, Lakim & Kandaung, 2008
Luperosaurus yasumai Ota, Sengoku & Hikida, 1996
Ptychozoon horsfieldii (Gray, 1827)
Ptychozoon kuhli Stejneger, 1902
Ptychozoon rhacophorus Boulenger, 1899

LACERTIDAE

Takydromus sexlineatus Daudin, 1802

LANTHANOTIDAE

Lanthanotus borneensis Steindachner, 1877

SCINCIDAE

Apterygodon vittatum Edeling, 1864
Brachymeles apus Hikida, 1982
Dasia grisea (Gray, 1845)
Dasia olivacea Gray, 1839
Dasia semicincta (Peters, 1867)
Emoia atrocostata (Lesson,1830)
Emoia caeruleocauda (De Vis, 1892)
Emoia cyanura (Lesson, 1830)
Eutropis indeprensa Brown & Alcala, 1980
Eutropis multifasciata (Kuhl, 1820)
Eutropis rudis Boulenger, 1887
Eutropis rugifera (Stoliczka, 1870)
Lamprolepis nieuwenhuisii (van Lidth de Jeude, 1905)
Lamprolepis vyneri (Shelford, 1905)
Larutia puehensis Grismer, Leong and Yaakob, 2003
Lipinia inexpectata Das and Austin, in press
Lipinia miangensis (Werner, 1910)
Lipinia nitens (Peters, 1871)

Lipinia vittigera
(Boulenger, 1894)
Lygosoma bampfyldei
(Bartlett, 1895)
Lygosoma bowringii
(Günther, 1864)
Sphenomorphus aesculeticola
Inger, Tan, Lakim &
Yambun, 2002
Sphenomorphus alfredi
(Boulenger, 1898)
Sphenomorphus buettikoferi
(van Lidth de Jeude, 1905)
Sphenomorphus crassa Inger,
Tan, Lakim & Yambun, 2002
Sphenomorphus cyanolaemus
Inger & Hosmer, 1965
Sphenomorphus haasi
Inger & Hosmer, 1965
Sphenomorphus hallieri
(van Lidth de Jeude, 1905)
Sphenomorphus kinabaluensis
(Bartlett, 1895)
Sphenomorphus maculicollus
Bacon, 1967
Sphenomorphus multisquamatus
Inger, 1958
Sphenomorphus murudensis
Smith, 1925
Sphenomorphus sabanus
Inger, 1958
Sphenomorphus shelfordi
(Boulenger, 1900)
Sphenomorphus stellatus
(Boulenger, 1900)
Sphenomorphus tanahtinggi
Inger, Tan, Lakim & Yambun,
2002
Sphenomorphus tenuiculus
(Mocquard, 1890)
Tropidophorus beccarii
Peters, 1871
Tropidophorus brookei
(Gray, 1845)
Tropidophorus iniquus
van Lidth de Jeude, 1905
Tropidophorus micropus
van Lidth de Jeude, 1905
Tropidophorus mocquardii
Boulenger, 1894
Tropidophorus perplexus
Barbour, 1921

VARANIDAE
Varanus dumerilii
(Schlegel, 1839)
Varanus rudicollis Gray, 1845
Varanus salvator
(Laurenti, 1768)

CROCODYLIDAE
Crocodylus porosus
Schneider, 1801
Crocodylus raninus
Müller & Schlegel, 1844
Tomistoma schlegelii
(Müller, 1838)

GAVIALIIDAE
Tomistoma schlegelii
(Müller, 1838)

DERMOCHELYIDAE
Dermochelys coriacea
(Vandelli, 1761)

CHELONIIDAE
Caretta caretta (Linnaeus, 1758)
Chelonia mydas (Linnaeus,1758)
Eretmochelys imbricata
(Linnaeus, 1766)
Lepidochelys olivacea
(Eschscholtz, 1829)

TRIONYCHIDAE
Amyda cartilaginea
(Boddaert, 1770)
Chitra chitra
Nutphand, 1979
Dogania subplana (Geoffroy-
Saint Hillaire, 1809)
Pelochelys cantorii Gray, 1864
**Pelodiscus sinensis*
(Wiegmann, 1835)

BATAGURIDAE
Batagur borneoensis
(Schlegel & Müller, 1844)
Cuora amboinensis Daudin, 1801
Cyclemys dentata (Gray, 1831)
Heosemys spinosa (Gray, 1831)
Notochelys platynota
(Gray, 1834)
Orlitia borneensis Gray, 1873
Siebenrockiella crassicollis
(Gray, 1831)

EMYDIDAE
**Trachemys scripta*
(Schoepff, 1792)

TESTUDINIDAE
Manouria emys (Schlegel &
Müller in: Temminck, 1844)

ACROCHORDIDAE (WART SNAKES)

Wart Snakes are stout, wrinkly-skinned aquatic snakes from the coastal waters of tropical Asia and Australasia. There are three species in the Asia-Pacific region, of which two occur in Borneo. All of them feed on fish. Sometimes, these species are killed for their skin or because of their fish-eating habits, by coastal dwellers.

Wart Snake *Acrochordus granulatus* 100cm

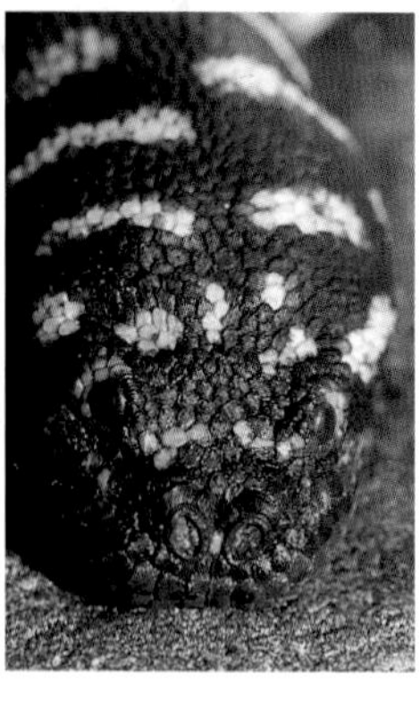

The Wart Snake and Elephant Trunk Snake are two closely related water snakes that, along with a third species from New Guinea, form a family of their own. They are thick-bodied snakes, lacking distinct ventral scales. The Wart Snake has a stout, compressed body and short, prehensile tail; head not distinct from neck and covered with small, juxtaposed scales; tiny eyes, with vertically elliptical pupils; a fold of skin present along middle of abdomen; rostrals absent; chin shields absent; midbody scale rows 100, with those on vertebral region being largest; a row of small scales separate large labial scales from mouth. The body is olive, blue or blackish-grey, with cream transverse bands that are best marked in juveniles, sometimes disappearing in adults. These snakes are estuarine and sometimes marine, feeding on other snakes. They are ovoviviparous, producing seven young, which measure 230mm. On Borneo, the species is known from Brunei, Sabah and Sarawak, the distribution of species including coastal India, Sri Lanka, Bangladesh, Myanmar, China, Thailand, the Malay Peninsula, Cambodia, the Philippines and western and central islands of Indonesia.

Elephant Trunk Snake *Acrochordus javanicus* 290cm

The Elephant Trunk Snake is identifiable from the Wart Snake (*Acrochordus granulatus*) in that it possesses a slightly compressed body and grows to over twice the size; scales on head are small and rough; midbody scale rows 120–150, of which those around the vertebrals are the largest. This species inhabits ditches and canals, in freshwater situations. Ovoviviparous, it produces clutches of 25–32 eggs. Hatchlings are 460mm. Within Borneo, it is known only from Brunei and Sarawak, although it is also suspected to occur in Sabah and in Kalimantan. The range of the species includes Peninsular Malaysia, Thailand, Cambodia, Vietnam, and some of the larger islands of western Indonesia.

Above: Close-up of skin.

PYTHONIDAE (PYTHONS)

The family of large constricting snakes are represented in Borneo by two species of pythons. They are stout-bodied snakes that lie in ambush for prey – comprising warm-bodied mammals and birds. Both species are in demand for their skin, and are also locally hunted for food and sometimes also, the pet trade.

Bornean Short Python *Python breitensteini* >2m

Above: close-up of head; below: close-up of midbody.

A small python; rostral broader than deep, with a deep pit on each side; loreals large; anterior pair of parietals in broad contact at median suture; postoculars 1–4; supralabials 9–11, two of them pitted; anterior and posterior infra-labials with weak pits; mid -body scale rows 53–57; ventrals 154–165; anal entire; subcaudals 27–33; dorsum is brown with rounded spots, that may be joined on vertebral region; sides with grey, dark-edged spots or wavy bands; pale head with a black line in centre, which is followed by pale spots that are black-edged; pale yellow or tan marking on body; sides of head with a broad dark band, through which is a pale transverse stripe running from eye to corner of mouth; cream venter, sometimes spotted with brown. Inhabits edges of waterbodies (such as sluggish rivers, swamps and marshes), in lowland tropical forests, where they ambush small mammals and birds. It is known to lay up to 12 eggs. Endemic to Borneo, this species is known from Brunei, Sabah and Sarawak, as well as Kalimantan.

Reticulated Python *Broghammerus reticulatus* >10m

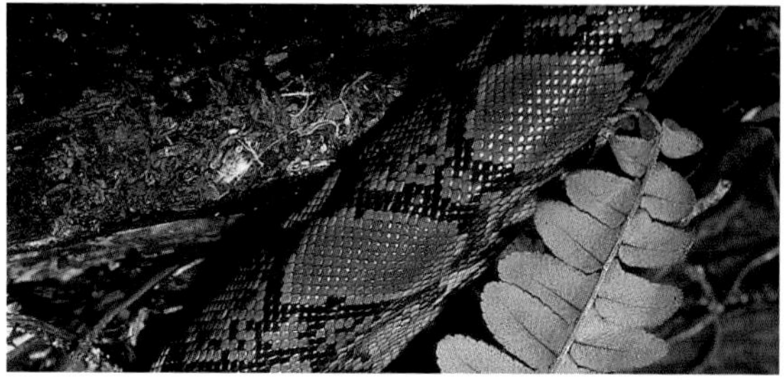

Above top: juvenile; above: close-up of midbody.

Above: close-up of adult.

This giant, constricting snake shares the title (and associated notoriety) of being the world's longest snake, along with the South American Anaconda (*Eunectes murinus*). However, the neo-tropical species is significantly heavier. Rostral is as broad as deep, visible from above; supralabials 12–14 , of which four anterior ones have pits and seventh or eighth enters orbit of eye; two or three anterior and five or six posterior infralabials with pits; 69–79 midbody scale rows; ventrals 297–330; anal single; subcaudals 78–102; dorsum is yellow or brown, with dark, rhomboidal markings; a black median line runs along forehead, from snout to nape; and an oblique line runs from posterior of eyes to corner of mouth; venter is yellow with small brown spots. This nocturnal species feeds on warm-blooded animals, such as mammals and birds. Large individuals are typically found at the water's edge, where they presumably lie in ambush for deer and pigs. Bornean records are from Brunei, Sabah, Sarawak as well as Kalimantan. Wide distribution, from Nicobar Islands, north-east India, Myanmar, Thailand, the Malay Peninsula, Vietnam, Laos, Cambodia and many of the islands of the Philippines and Indonesia.

COLUBRIDAE ('TYPICAL' SNAKES)

The so-called 'typical snakes' include a huge assemblage (worldwide with nearly 2,000 species) of snakes, which vary in their mode of life, from burrowing to terrestrial forms, arboreal to aquatic types. There is, thus, nothing typical about this group, and the name derives from the fact that most of the common (and once best known) snakes of Europe belong to this family. Although a majority of these species are harmless, a few have proven to have lethal bites, such as some of keelback snakes; while others, with their enlarged teeth, such as cat snakes and kukri snakes, need to be handled with care.

Speckled-headed Vine Snake *Ahaetulla fasciolata* 169cm

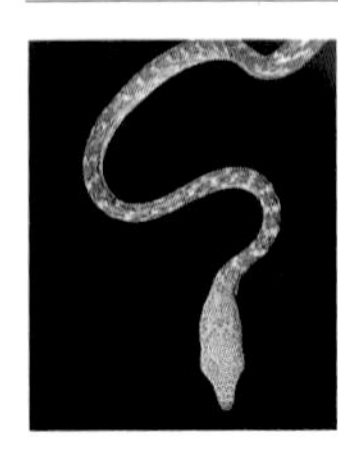

A brown or pinkish-tan tree snake. Body slender; snout long, ending in a curled rostral scale; eyes large with a horizontal pupil; long, thin tail; midbody scale rows 15; vertebral scale row enlarged; ventrals 194–235; dorsum light brown or pinkish-tan, with numerous narrow, oblique dark bands on the anterior of body; forehead with elongated or curved dark markings; dark grey venter. Inhabiting forested and semi-urban habitats, it has a wide altitudinal range, from sea level up to ca.900m. Feeds on lizards and frogs, and is reportedly ovoviviparous, although further biological details are lacking. The Bornean distribution of species includes Brunei, Sarawak, Kalimantan and Sabah; it is also known from Thailand, the Malay Peninsula, to Sumatra and the Natuna and Riau Archipelagos.

Oriental Vine Snake *Ahaetulla prasina* 197cm

A bright green, long-nosed tree snake, likely to be seen in lightly forested areas, including parks and gardens. Elongated snout; tail over a third head and body length; eye with a horizontal pupil and a groove along snout, before eyes; midbody scale rows 15; ventrals 194–235; subcaudals 154–207; dorsum of this typically green snake can also be brown and there is a yellow stripe along each side of body; venter light green. A forest-dwelling snake, found on low vegetation, such as shrubs and saplings, it also comes into parks and gardens in search of lizards and birds. Usually aggressive and quick to bite, it has a **mildly toxic saliva**. A threat display comprises expanding its neck to reveal black and white skin between scales. Curious among snakes is the habit of these snakes to stick their tongue out of their mouth for a long time. Ovoviviparous, it produces 4–6 live ones that are light brown in colour. Within Borneo, this snake has been reported from Brunei, Sarawak and Sabah as well as Kalimantan. A large global distribution from north-eastern India, Bhutan and Bangladesh, through Myanmar, Thailand, China, Laos, Cambodia, Vietnam, the Malay Peninsula, to the islands of western and central Indonesia and the Philippines.

White-fronted Water Snake *Amphiesma flavifrons* 750mm

A frequently-encountered water snake, seen swimming in rivers in the plains and midhills. Body slender; midbody scales 19, keeled; ventrals 149–157; subcaudals 92–101; dorsum olive-grey, with darker markings; a distinctive white to yellowish-cream spot on snout; juveniles with paired white spots along midback; venter cream with an alternating series of black spots. Often seen swimming along rivers, with its head held out of water, its diet includes frogs, tadpoles and frog eggs. Its reproductive biology remains unknown. The species is known from Brunei, Sabah and Sarawak, and is endemic to Borneo.

Sarawak Grass Snake *Amphiesma sarawacense* 780mm

A lowland and sub-montane snake from Borneo. Slender snake; tail long; midbody scale rows 17, keeled; ventrals 134–154; subcaudals 52–112; dorsum olive to reddish-brown, the back with black squarish markings; a row of light spots on flanks; upper lip yellow or cream. Inhabits primary forests, in the plains, and hills up to 1,700m, concealing itself under fallen logs. It hunts for frogs and frog eggs in streams. Produces clutches of 4–5 eggs. Nothing else is known of its biology. This snake is known from Brunei, Sarawak and Sabah, and has also been reported from the highlands of Peninsular Malaysia.

Blunt-headed Tree Snake *Aplopeltura boa* 850mm

A large-headed, arboreal snake with enormous eyes. Body remarkably slender, laterally compressed; head blunt, wider than body; eyes large; tail about a third body length; midbody scale rows 13; ventrals 148–191; subcaudals 88–131; dorsum brown to greyish-brown, typically with dark-edged saddle-like markings; flanks often with white spots; lips cream; a cream patch under eye. Inhabits lowland forests, up to about 1,500m, and active at night on low vegetation, where it hunts lizards and perhaps also snails. Between 4–5 eggs are produced at a time. The Bornean records are from Sabah and Sarawak, but not Kalimantan. The distribution of this species includes Myanmar, Thailand, West Malaysia, the Philippines and islands of western Indonesia.

Smooth Slug-eating Snake *Asthenodipsas laevis* 600mm

A small, smooth-scaled snake from lowlands that, like the previous species, eats snails. Body slender, laterally compressed; tail short; midbody scale rows 15, smooth; midline of back with a keel; scales on vertebral region slightly enlarged; ventrals 148–178; subcaudals 34–69; dorsum brown with numerous dark vertical bars; venter cream or pale yellow, edges of each scale with a dark spot. An essentially lowland species, it has been found as high as 1,150m. It is active at night on low vegetation, where it hunts slugs and snails. Its reproductive biology remains unknown. Within Borneo, this species is known from Sarawak, Sabah and Kalimantan, and extralimitally, from Java.

Dog-toothed Cat Snake *Boiga cynodon* 280cm

A large cat snake. Body large but relatively slender, distinctly compressed; midbody scales 23–25; vertebrals distinctly enlarged; ventrals 248–290; subcaudals 114–165; dorsum brownish-tan, with dark brown or reddish-brown bands, that darkens posteriorly; a dark postocular stripe; juveniles lighter. Inhabits lowland forests and edges. Its diet comprises small vertebrates, primarily birds and their eggs, and more rarely, small mammals and lizards. Clutches include 6–12 eggs, and several clutches may be laid at a time. Known from Sabah, Sarawak and Kalimantan, this species is also distributed in the Malay Peninsula, Sumatra, Java, the Lesser Sunda Islands and the Philippines.

Mangrove Cat Snake *Boiga dendrophila* 250cm

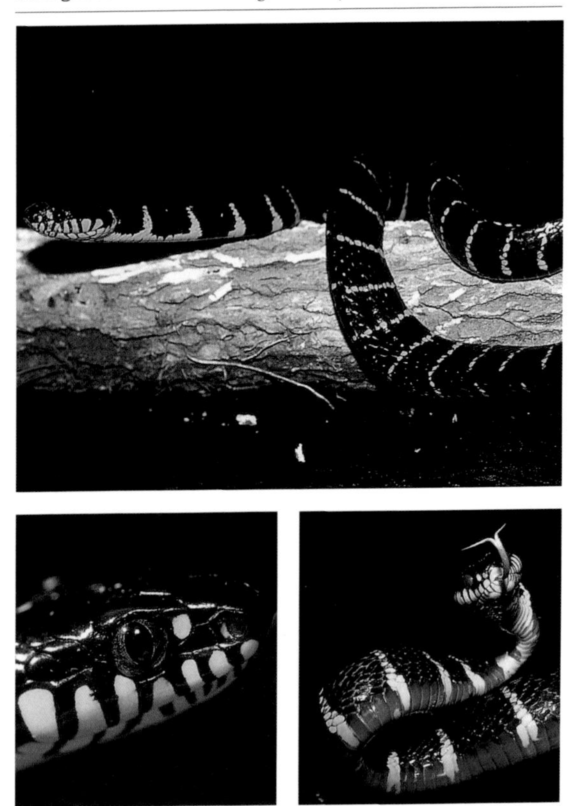

A large, unmistakable, ringed cat snake. Body large, robust; eyes large; midbody scale rows 21; ventrals 221–253; subcaudals 89–118; dorsum black with 35–45 narrow yellow rings around body and tail; venter grey; throat and lips are yellow. Inhabits lowland forests, including mangrove swamps, where it is generally found resting on trees. It consumes birds, including their eggs and nestlings, amphibians, lizards, other snakes, and even small mammals (such as mouse deer and tree shrews), the largest prey recorded being mouse deer or chevrotain. Clutches of 4–15 eggs, measuring 45.5–51 x 24.5–25mm are produced at a time, hatching in about 90 days to produce young ones measuring 340mm. **Its saliva is suspected to be toxic**, although it belongs to a family of otherwise essentially non-venomous snakes, and therefore, this snake deserves to be treated with appropriate caution. Widespread in Borneo, with records from Brunei, Sabah, Sarawak and Kalimantan, the distribution of this snake, in eight subspecies, is large – from Thailand, the Malay Peninsula, Vietnam, the Philippines and western and central Indonesia, including Sulawesi.

White-spotted Cat Snake *Boiga drapiezii* 210cm

An arboreal species from lowland forests and swamps, it feeds on small vertebrates. Body long and slender; midbody scale rows 19; ventrals 258–287; subcaudals 150–173; dorsum variable, ranging from olive-grey to reddish-brown; vertebral region with paired pink spots anteriorly, that fuse to form a line; pink or cream spots on flanks; forehead with dark speckling. Inhabits lowland forests up to 1,000m. Diet comprises birds, bird eggs, frogs, lizards and large insects. Eggs are laid in termite-infested wood. Known from Brunei, Sabah and Sarawak, but not Kalimantan. Outside of Borneo, this species has been reported from Thailand, the Malay Peninsula, to the western and central islands of Indonesia and the Philippines.

Jasper Cat Snake *Boiga jaspidea* 150cm

A small, brightly-coloured cat snake. Body slender, laterally compressed; head large, distinct from neck; midbody scale rows 21; ventrals 243–267; subcaudals 140–166; dorsum brown, reddish-brown or grey-brown, with twin row of dark spots or bars on the flanks and a greyish-red vertebral stripe. Known from lowland forests and peat swamps. It is a predator of small vertebrates, specializing in geckos and other lizards, although small mammals, birds, bird eggs and snakes are also consumed. Eggs may be deposited in nests of tree-dwelling termites, numbering six, of dimensions 38–39 x 18–19mm. Hatchlings measure 390–400mm. Recorded from Brunei, Sabah, Sarawak and Kalimantan, this snake is also known from the Malay Peninsula to Borneo, Sumatra and Java.

Black-headed Cat Snake *Boiga nigriceps* 200cm

A black-capped cat snake. Body fairly robust, laterally compressed; midbody scale rows 21, smooth; ventrals 246–293; subcaudals 137–148; dorsum brown to olive-brown; forehead often darker, as is the tail; lips cream or yellow; venter cream, darkening posteriorly. Inhabits lowland forests and is presumably arboreal. Its diet includes birds and other snakes. Nothing is known of its reproductive biology. A back-fanged snake that needs to be treated with caution, as **envenomations from its bite have been reported**. Known from Sabah and Sarawak, extralimital populations have been found on Peninsular Malaysia, Sumatra and Java.

Bicoloured Reed Snake *Calamaria bicolor* 450mm

A bicoloured slender snake. Body slender; tail thick, tapering from base; preocular scale present; nasal pointed forward; third and fourth supralabials enter orbit of eye; ventrals 139–169; subcaudals 18–28; dorsum blue-black or dark brown, unpatterned or with dark cross-bands; venter typically unpatterned yellow, sometimes spotted with black. A terrestrial snake from the midhills up to submontane limits. Its diet and reproductive habits are unstudied. Recorded from Sabah, Sarawak and Kalimantan. Outside of Borneo, this species is known from Java.

Grabowsky's Reed Snake *Calamaria grabowskyi* 468mm

A small lowland and montane species of reed snake. Body slender; head slightly distinct from neck; tail long, tapering; third and fourth supralabials enter eye; ventrals 150–190; subcaudals 20–29; dorsum dark brown, each scale with a dark network; scattered dark brown or yellow spots on back; lips yellow; lateral bands composed of elongated dark spots. Inhabits primary forests of northern Sabah, its diet and reproductive biology remain unstudied. Known from elevations of around 1,000m from the mountains of Sabah, Sarawak and Kalimantan, and is endemic to Borneo.

White-bellied Reed Snake *Calamaria leucogaster* 223mm

A brightly-coloured reed snake, with half rings on neck and around tail base. Body slender; head slightly distinct from neck; tail tapers to a narrow point; third and fourth supralabials enter orbit of eye; mental does not contact anterior chin shield; ventrals 126–157; subcaudals 12–26; dorsum highly variable, ranging from bright orange-red, through olive to brown, typically with dark longitudinal stripes; a black collar, 3–5 scales wide; venter cream-coloured. Almost nothing is known of the biology of this lowland species, except that it dwells on the forest floor, hiding under logs by day. Known from Brunei, Sabah, Sarawak and Kalimantan, in Borneo, as well as Sumatra.

Variable Reed Snake *Calamaria lumbricoidea* 500mm

A red-headed snake that may possibly mimic venomous snakes, such as the Red-headed Krait or the Malayan Striped Coral Snake. Head blunt; tail short, tapering; midbody scale rows 13, smooth; ventrals 137–199; subcaudals 14–26; dorsum black with narrow cream or yellow rings; head red in juveniles, turning black with growth; venter yellow with black ventral scales forming bands. Associated with lowland forests and gardens, it lives in the leaf litter. Diet comprises earthworms. Its reproductive habits are unknown. Recorded from Sabah, Sarawak and Kalimantan, it is widespread in Sundaland, including Peninsular Malaysia, Borneo and Java, also occurring in the Philippines.

Red-headed Reed Snake *Calamaria schlegelii* 395mm

A lowland representative of the genus. Body slender; tail long and tapering; nasal as large as eye; third and fourth supralabials enter orbit of eye; ventrals 130–180; subcaudals 19–44; dorsum dark brown or black; head red, orange or yellow; venter unpatterned yellow. A lowland forest species, found on the leaf litter. Its diet comprises frogs and slugs. Of its reproductive habits, nothing is known, except that it produces eggs. Recorded from Sabah and Sarawak, but not Kalimantan, the distribution of this species extends from the Malay Peninsula to Sumatra, Borneo and Java; the population from Java is allocated to another subspecies.

Schmidt's Reed Snake *Calamaria schmidti* 280mm.

A Kinabalu endemic species of reed snake. Body slender; tail short, ending in a blunt point; four supralabials; supralabials II and III entering orbit of eye; preocular absent; mental not touching chin shield; ventrals 127–150; subcaudals 14–22; dorsum unpatterned blackish-grey, with green and blue iridescence, scales with a pale margin; venter light grey or yellow, darkening to purple posteriorly. Inhabits montane forests, where it hides under fallen logs by day, and is active on the ground, besides streams at night. Apart from the discovery of an earthworm from the stomach of one specimen, nothing is known of its diet. Known records of this species include Bundu Tuhan and the Kinabalu Park Headquarters area, at 1,370–1,570m.

Dog-faced Water Snake *Cerberus rynchops* 100cm

A water snake with a projecting upper jaw, giving it a dog-like appearance. Head long and distinct from neck; eyes small and beady, with rounded pupil; midbody scale rows 23 or 25, distinctly keeled; ventrals 136–160; subcaudals 51–69; dorsum dark grey, with faint dark blotches and a dark line along sides of head, across eyes; venter yellowish-cream, with dark grey areas. Abundant in low-lying areas, such as mangrove mudflats and rice fields, where they hide in crab holes, emerging at night to feed. Diet comprises fishes, such as mudskippers and gobies, as well as crabs and frogs. Between 6–30 young ones are born at a time, which remain together for a while before dispersing. Bornean records are from Sabah and Sarawak, as well as Kalimantan. This snake has an enormous distribution, with three subspecies (considered species by some authorities) that range from India, eastwards to Australia.

Garden Flying Snake *Chrysopelea paradisi* 1.5m

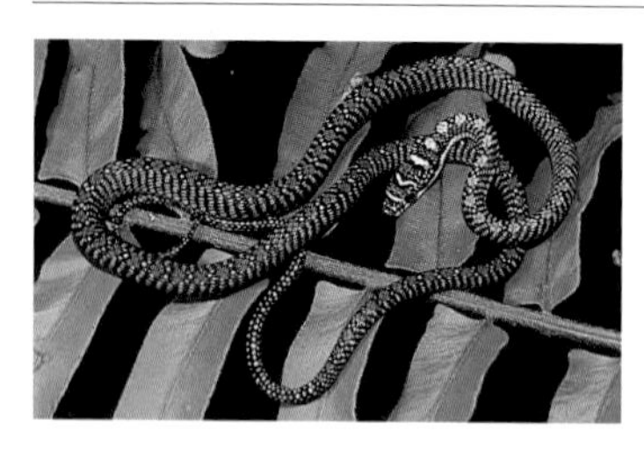

This is the familiar 'flying' snake of Borneo – a brightly-coloured tree snake. Head distinct from neck and flattened; eyes rounded and bulge out; scales smooth; tail relatively long; midbody scale rows 17; ventrals 218–239; subcaudals 118–137; head and body black, centre of each scale with a green spot; vertebral region with a row of 3–4 pink or red spots; forehead with yellow bands; venter green, with black edges. Inhabits forested habitats in lowlands in South-east Asia, occasionally entering human habitation. Highly arboreal and capable of extended leaps between treetops, when body is flattened into a ribbon-like shape, allowing it to glide for considerable distances. It has a **mild venom** and its diet includes lizards, such as geckos. Clutches of five eggs are produced at a time. Within Borneo, it is known from Brunei, Sabah and Sarawak, but not Kalimantan. This species has a wide distribution, from Narcondum Island in Andaman Archipelago, east through Thailand, the Malay Peninsula, Sumatra, Borneo and Java.

Twin-barred Flying Snake *Chrysopelea pelias* 70cm

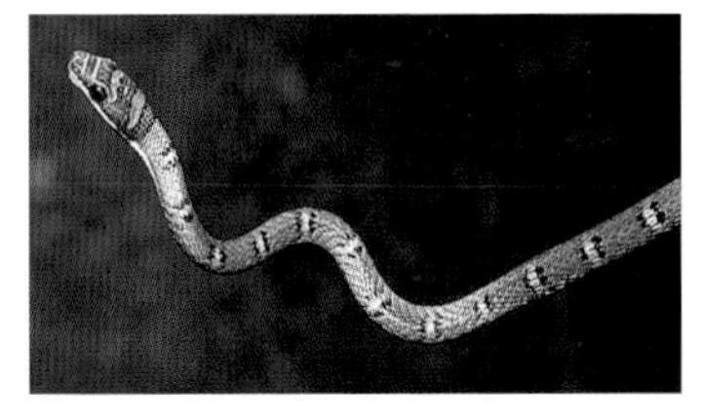

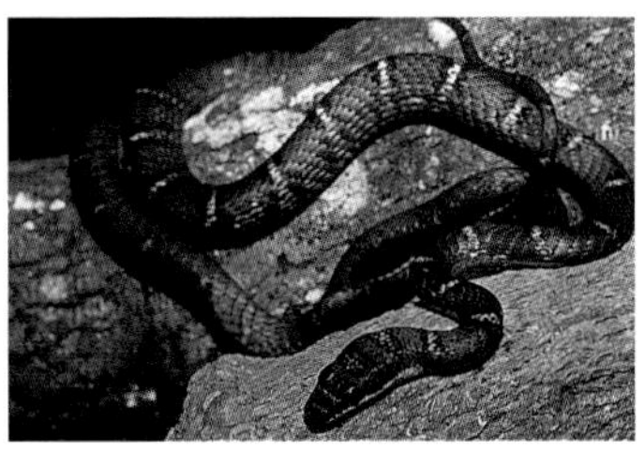

Another arboreal snake, this too inhabits lowland forests and on occasions, may enter human habitations. Head distinct from neck and flattened; midbody scale rows 17; ventrals 181–199; subcaudals 111–120; dorsum with red triangular areas separated by paired black bars; forehead brown, with three red cross-bars. A gliding and parachuting snake, it is associated with lowlands, from near sea level to about 600m. Its diet comprises lizards; its breeding habits are unknown. Within Borneo, known from Brunei, Sabah and Sarawak, but not Kalimantan. Its distribution outside Borneo includes Myanmar, Thailand, the Malay Peninsula, Sumatra, Mentawai, Natuna and Riau Archipelagos and Java.

Common Malayan Racer *Coelognathus flavolineatus* 180cm

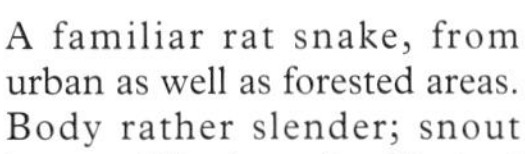

A familiar rat snake, from urban as well as forested areas. Body rather slender; snout long; midbody scales 19, keeled; ventrals 193–234; subcaudals 89–115; tail about one quarter snout-vent length; dorsum brownish-grey, with a dark stripe from behind eye to above back of mouth, and another one along nape; several short dark stripes or elongated blotches present on top and sides of body. Terrestrial and arboreal, inhabiting forested areas in lowlands and disturbed habitats, such as parks and gardens. However, it enters water freely. Its diet includes rodents and birds, as well as frogs and lizards. Clutches of 5–12 eggs are produced, that take 75–90 days to hatch. Bornean records of this species are from Brunei, Sarawak, Sabah and Kalimantan. It is widespread in distribution, with a range from Andaman Islands of India, east through Thailand, the Malay Peninsula, Vietnam, to Sumatra, Borneo and Java.

Copperhead Racer *Coelognathus radiatus* 230cm

A brightly-coloured rat-eating snake from the lowlands and midhills. Body relatively slender; head narrow; tail short, slender; midbody scale rows 19; anal scale undivided; ventrals 222–250; subcaudals 82–108; anal entire; dorsum greyish-brown; a thin dark line from eye to lip; a broad black line from eye to back of head, where it joins a line running across the back of the head. Associated with lowlands and midhills, from forests and open areas, up to 1,400m. Frogs and rodents comprise their diets. Up to six eggs are produced several times a year, hatchlings 250–300mm emerging after 64–95 days. Within Borneo, only known from Kalimantan, the range of the species is large, extending from India and southern China, to Myanmar, Thailand, Vietnam, Cambodia, Laos, the Malay Peninsula, Sumatra, Borneo and Java.

Striped Bronzeback Tree Snake *Dendrelaphis caudolineatus* 152cm

An arboreal species, it also shows a lot of terrestrial activity, for which reason it is frequently found as a road-kill. Body slender; head wider than neck; snout bluntly-rounded; tail long, eyes large; midbody scale rows 13, smooth; ventrals 174–189; subcaudals 105–116; both ventrals and subcaudals with a sharp keel on their outer edges; dorsum olive-brown; a pale green stripe on the lower flanks, edged on top by a narrow black stripe, and on the bottom, by a broad black stripe; all stripes most conspicuous on the tail; venter pale green. Associated with lowlands and encountered in forests as well as in parks and gardens, typically on shrubs, but ascends to hunt prey, such as frogs and lizards. Between 5–8 eggs are produced at a time, measuring 12 x 48mm, that, after an incubation period of 54 days, produce 340mm hatchlings. Within Borneo, this species has been recorded from Brunei, Sabah and Sarawak as well as Kalimantan. Its extralimital distribution includes Myanmar, Thailand, the Malay Peninsula, the Philippines, Sumatra, the Mentawai and Riau Archipelagos, and probably Java.

Kopstein's Bronzeback Tree Snake *Dendrelaphis kopsteini* 143cm

Body slender; head distinct from neck; 2 supralabials touch orbit; single loreal; eye moderate; pupil rounded; vertebral scales larger than lowest dorsal row; midbody scale rows 15; ventrals 167–181; subcaudals 140–154, paired; anal divided. Dorsum bronze brown; black postocular stripe across lower half of temporal region to end of jaw; vertebral scales with broad black posterior margin; interstitial skin on anterior of body brick-red; venter grey. Lowland dipterocarp forests, up to 700m asl. Diurnal and arboreal. Diet includes geckos. Oviparous, producing eight eggs. Incubation period 92 days. Hatchlings 270–300mm. Borneo (Brunei). Also, southern Thailand, Peninsular Malaysia, Singapore, Sumatra and the Mentawai Archipelago.

Painted Bronzeback Tree Snake *Dendrelaphis pictus* 125cm

A familiar tree snake from parks and gardens, and one that sometimes enters houses. Head distinct from neck; eyes large with rounded pupils; midbody scales 15, smooth; ventrals 169–194; subcaudals 130–151; iris golden; dorsum bronze-brown or brownish-olive, with a yellow or cream stripe, edged with black along flanks; forehead brown with a black lateral stripe from nasal to neck; blue or greenish-blue skin patch on neck that are displayed when excited. Inhabits forested areas, but will also come into plantations and around human habitation. When molested, it exudes a foul-smelling musk from its anal glands. Diurnal and arboreal, it hunts frogs and lizards. Clutches comprise 3–8 eggs, measuring 22–38.5 x 8.5–11mm, and several clutches may be produced a year. Hatchlings measure 280mm. Inhabits forested as well as grassy areas from sea level to over 1,330m. On Borneo, it has been recorded from Brunei, Sabah and Sarawak as well as Kalimantan. Otherwise, distributed from India and eastern China to South-east Asia.

Half-banded Bridled Snake *Dryocalamus subannulatus* 600mm

A slender-bodied, smooth-scaled snake that specializes in eating lizards and frogs. Head distinct from neck; a single preocular; eyes large; pupil vertical; midbody scale rows 15; ventrals 225–244; subcaudals 88–107; anal entire; dorsum tan or light brown, with large brown spots; on flanks, a smaller spot; two streaks along eyes; venter yellow. Associated with lowland forests and disturbed areas, it can climb low vegetation when hunting small vertebrates. Its reproductive biology is unknown. Within Borneo, this species is known from the suburbs of Bandar Seri Begawan, in Brunei, and Sandakan in Sabah. Its range also includes Thailand, the Malay Peninsula, Palawan in the Philippines, Sumatra and the Mentawai and Riau Archipelagos.

Three-banded Bridled Snake *Dryocalamus tristrigatus* 650mm

A related species, it can be distinguished from the previous species in showing the absence of preoculars. Head distinct from neck; eyes large; pupil vertical; midbody scale rows 15; ventrals 218–231; subcaudals 86–96; anal entire; dorsum dark brown, with three white stripes; head shields with a white edge; upper lip white; venter cream. Inhabits lowland forests. Known to feed on lizards, it forages in the evenings along rocky areas as well as up trees. Its breeding habits are unknown. Recorded from Sabah and Sarawak, but not from Kalimantan. It has a relatively small range outside of Borneo – Natuna Islands and some of the southern islands of the Philippines (Balabac and Palawan).

Keel-bellied Whip Snake *Dryophiops rubescens* 540mm

A reddish-brown arboreal snake, from lowland forests. Head distinct from neck; eyes large; pupil horizontal; midbody scale rows 15; ventrals 186–199; subcaudals 111–136; anal divided; dorsum reddish-brown, with small black spots; a dark streak on head; venter yellow or olive. Inhabits lowland forests and found on low vegetation as well as low branches of trees and active by day. It feeds on lizards and produces 2–3 eggs at a time. Recorded from Sabah and Sarawak, the range of the species extends from Thailand and the Malay Peninsula, to Sumatra, Java and the Mentawai Archipelago.

Dark Grey Ground Snake *Elapoidis fusca* 500mm

A wet zone snake, known from submontane forests. Head indistinct from neck; eyes reduced; pupil rounded; snout short; midbody scale rows 15, keeled; ventrals 146–158; subcaudals 74–91; anal entire; dorsum dark brown, unpatterned or with yellow spots; sometimes, anterior of body yellow with a dark brown vertebral stripe and dark spots on flanks; venter yellow. A hill snake, which, on Sumatra and Java, is found at elevations of over 1,000m. Nothing is known of its diet or reproduction. Distributed in Java and Sumatra, the sole record from Borneo is from Sabah, without a precise locality.

Common Smooth Water Snake *Enhydris enhydris* 810mm

A common water snake from southern and south-eastern Asia. Head rather small, body medium-sized, body stout and cylindrical; head somewhat depressed and only slightly distinct from neck; snout rounded; nostrils situated on upper surface of head; pupils vertical; dorsal scales smooth, lacking apical pits; midbody scale rows 21; ventrals 141–174; dorsum greyish-brown or olive-green, typically with a dark vertebral and two light lateral stripes from upper surface of head to tail; venter yellowish-cream, with a dark line along each side. Inhabits freshwater and sometimes also, brackish water areas, including slow-moving rivers, marshes, lakes and wet ricefields. Diet comprises fishes, frogs and tadpoles, and sometimes lizards. Ovoviviparous, producing several clutches a year, each comprising 4–20 young that measure 155mm. Known from Sarawak and Kalimantan, in Borneo, this snake is widespread, from eastern India, besides Nepal, Bangladesh, southern China, Myanmar, Thailand, Vietnam, the Malay Peninsula, Sumatra, Java and Borneo.

Plumbeous Water Snake *Enhydris plumbea* 480mm

A dark-coloured water snake, associated with swamps and ditches. Body cylindrical in cross-section; two postoculars; tail short and compressed; midbody scale rows 19; ventrals 112–139; subcaudals 29–43; dorsum greyish-olive, each scale with a dark brown or black edge; upper lips and venter cream or yellow, the latter with black spots. Inhabits wetlands, such as swamps, marshes, buffalo wallows, streams and ditches, and sometimes, even estuaries and back waters, its diet includes frogs, frog eggs and tadpoles, besides fishes. Between June and November, 6–30 young ones, measuring 75–115mm are born. Bornean records of the species include Brunei, Sabah and Kalimantan. Widespread from southern China, Vietnam, through Myanmar, Thailand, the Malay Peninsula to Borneo, Sumatra, Java, Bali and northern Sulawesi.

White-bellied Mangrove Snake *Fordonia leucobalia* 950mm

An extremely variable water snake in terms of colouration, found in mangrove areas and other riverine areas adjacent to the sea. Head short, wide, scarcely wider than neck; head scales large and distinct; loreal absent; lower jaw short; enlarged rear fangs present; midbody scales 25–29, smooth; ventrals 137–159; subcaudals 27–43; dorsum colouration and pattern variable, and within a locality, may be dark grey or brown, with light spots, or light grey, yellow or orange with dark spots; venter pale cream, sometimes with small dark spots; lips yellowish-cream. Inhabits tidal portions of rivers. Crabs form the dietary mainstay, although small fishes and mud lobsters are also consumed. Ovoviviparous, producing 10–15 young at a time; hatchlings measure 180mm. This coastal species is known from Sarawak, within Borneo, and extralimital populations are known from India's Andaman Islands, Myanmar, the Malay Peninsula, Sumatra, Java, Borneo, Lesser Sundas, the Philippines, east to New Guinea and northern Australia.

Orange-bellied Snake *Gongylosoma baliodeirum* 450mm

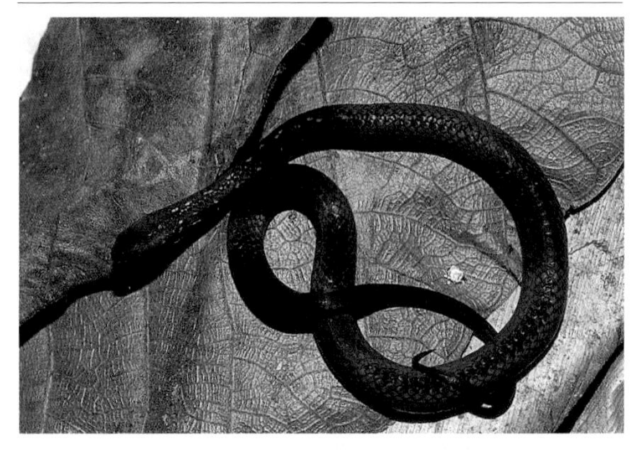

A common but poorly-known ground-dwelling snake. A small snake; head slightly wider than neck; midbody scale rows 13, smooth; ventrals 118–141; subcaudals 58–75; anal divided; dorsum dark brown to reddish-brown, with paired rows of cream spots; upper labials edged with dark grey; venter yellowish-cream, sometimes with fine dark spots. Associated with a variety of habitats, from lowlands to submontane limits (up to 1,500m), this terrestrial snake hides under fallen logs and stones during the day. Spiders, other arthropods and lizards have been recorded in its diet, and its reproductive habits are unknown, although it is suspected to be oviparous. The Bornean records of this species include Brunei, Sarawak, Sabah and Kalimantan. Besides Borneo, this snake is known from Thailand, the Malay Peninsula, Sumatra and Java.

Striped Ground Snake *Gongylosoma longicauda* 500mm

Another small ground-dwelling snake. Head wider than neck; tail long and slender; midbody scale rows 13, smooth; ventrals 124–138; subcaudals 92–105; anal divided; dorsum brownish-red, with a yellow or cream chevron at the back of its head and five light stripes on back, best marked on the anterior of body; venter unpatterned cream. Inhabits lowland rainforests, and feeds on spiders. Its breeding habits are unknown. Recorded from Sabah and Sarawak, this species is also known from Sumatra and Java.

Brown-tailed Racer *Gonyosoma oxycephalum* 240cm

A beautiful green snake, typically with a brown tail (red in some populations outside Borneo). The head is elongated, squarish, coffin-shaped; body rather thick-set; midbody scale rows 23, 25 or 27, feebly keeled or smooth; ventrals 236–262; subcaudals 130–149; dorsum emerald-green, with a light green throat and a black stripe along sides of head, across eyes; venter yellow; juveniles are olive-brown with narrow white bars towards back of body. Inhabits lowland forests; arboreal and perhaps also frequently terrestrial, judging from road-killed individuals. Diet includes rats and squirrels, as well as birds. Several clutches are produced annually, eggs numbering 5–12, 65mm in length, and take 100–120 days to hatch. Within Borneo, this species has been recorded from Brunei, Sabah, Sarawak and Kalimantan. It has a wide extralimital distribution, from Andaman Islands of India, east through Thailand, Malaya, Indonesia and the Philippines.

Puff-faced Water Snake *Homalopsis buccata* 140cm

A medium-sized aquatic snake with a swollen face. Head large and distinct from neck; eyes and nostrils directed upward, snout squarish; eyes small; pupils vertically oval; body flattened dorso-ventrally; each scale distinctly keeled; ventrals 155–174; subcaudals 68–101; dorsum dark brown to black, with 19–51 narrow yellow, black-edged cross-bars. Inhabits slow moving and stagnant waterways, such as swamps, ponds and ricefields. They are **mildly venomous, and bite viciously when caught**. Active both by day and at night, when they forage by ambush for fish, and rarely, crustaceans and frogs. Breeding may be continuous, with gravid females and neonates found throughout the year. Ovoviviparous, 2–20 young ones being produced at a time; the newborn measures 143–230mm. Within Borneo, known from Sarawak and Kalimantan, this species is distributed from eastern India, eastwards to Myanmar, Thailand, Vietnam, the Malay Peninsula, Sumatra, Java and Borneo.

Yellow-spotted Water Snake *Hydrablabes periops* 530mm

A water snake, from the lowlands and midhills. A small snake; tail short; head small and narrower than body; eye small, with a rounded pupil and separated from upper lips by a ring of small scales; midbody scale rows 15 or 17, smooth; ventrals 179–209; subcaudals 56–76; anal divided; dorsum olive-brown, some individuals with a pale brown stripe on flanks; others are unpatterned; venter yellow or grey. An aquatic species, associated with streams, from the plains to the low hills (150–600m). Its diet and reproductive habits remain unstudied. Recorded from Brunei, Sarawak and Sabah, as well as Kalimantan, this snake is an endemic of Borneo.

Slender-tailed Wolf Snake *Lepturophis borneensis* 200cm

Above: adult; right: close-up; below: juvenile.

A large, slender wolf snake. Head wider than neck; snout short, blunt and depressed; pupil vertical; tail long; midbody scale rows 17, keeled; ventrals 225–259; subcaudals 171–206; anal divided; dorsum unpatterned dark brown or brownish-black in adults; juveniles have 30–40 narrow white or yellow bands on dorsum; venter unpatterned cream. A lowland species, typically associated with streams, from sea level to about 500m, it inhabits relatively open forests, and from its long tail, appears to have some arboreal activity. Diet is composed mainly of lizards and frogs. Its reproductive habits are unknown. Known from Sabah and Sarawak within Borneo, the range of the species includes Peninsular Malaysia.

Three-coloured Ring-necked Snake *Liopeltis tricolor* 56cm

A slender, arboreal snake. Head hardly distinct from neck; snout long; pupils rounded; tail long; midbody scale rows 15, smooth; ventrals 140–187; subcaudals 103–137; anal divided; dorsum yellowish-olive; a dark streak along eyes to beyond neck; venter yellowish-cream, with an olive streak on sides of each scale. Inhabits lowland forests, its dietary and reproductive biology remain unknown. Bornean records of the species are from Brunei, Sabah and Sarawak. The species also known from the Malay Peninsula, Sumatra and the Mentawai Archipelago.

Brown Wolf Snake *Lycodon effraenis* 100cm

A widespread but poorly-known wolf snake. Body slender; head flattened; rounded snout; loreal absent; midbody scales 17, smooth; ventrals 215–233; subcaudals 75–99; anal entire; dorsum reddish-brown or dark brown; three yellow rings encircling the body that disappear in older individuals; juveniles also with yellow streaks on sides of head; venter unpatterned brown. Inhabits lowland forests, from sea level to about 700m and seems tolerant of disturbance, turning up in human dwellings. Its diet presumably comprises lizards and small snakes. Reproductive habits unknown. Bornean records are from Sarawak and Kalimantan. Distributed from Peninsular Malaysia to Sumatra and Borneo.

Blue-necked Water Snake *Macropisthodon rhodomelas* 75cm

A frog-eating snake, associated with wetlands. midbody scale rows 19, keeled; ventrals 124–138; subcaudals 42–58; dorsum reddish-brown, with a black vertebral stripe that enters the nape as an inverted chevron; outside this, the neck is light blue; venter pink, each ventral scale with a small dark spot. Inhabits streams and other wetlands in the lowlands. When alarmed, it raises its head and flattens its neck – a behaviour reminiscent of a cobra, and at the same time, may discharge a white secretion from the nuchal gland. Diet comprises frogs and toads, and juveniles of these snakes will also consume tadpoles. Reproductive habits little known, except that clutches comprise 25 eggs. Besides Borneo, where it has been found in Sarawak and Sabah, it is known from southern Thailand, Peninsular Malaysia, Sumatra and Java.

Eight-lined Kukri Snake *Oligodon octolineatus* 700mm

An egg-eating snake. Head short, scarcely distinct from neck; eyes small, pupil rounded; two anterior temporals; midbody scale rows 17; ventrals 155–197; subcaudals 43–61; brown or reddish-brown, with 5–7 light longitudinal stripes, bordered by 6–8 dark stripes; forehead with two black stripes; venter yellow. Inhabits lowland forests, and active on the ground as well as on vegetation. Apart from bird eggs, it also feeds on frogs, their eggs, lizards and other snakes. Clutches of 4–5 eggs, measuring 16 x 30mm are laid at a time. Within Borneo, the species has been recorded from Brunei, Sarawak, Sabah and Kalimantan. Outside of Borneo, it is known from the Malay Peninsula, Sumatra, the Mentawai Archipelago, Bangka, Belitung, Java, the Riau and Sulu Archipelagos and Sulawesi.

Purple Kukri Snake *Oligodon purpurascens* 900mm

Another egg-eating snake. Head short, scarcely distinct from neck; eyes small, pupil rounded; midbody scale rows 19 or 21; ventrals 160–210; subcaudals 40–60; anal entire; dorsum brownish-purple, with dark, wavy bands or yellow transverse bands; a dark chevron-like marking on forehead; venter pink or red, with dark, squarish spots. Ground-dwelling in lowland forests, from sea level up to about 1,200m. Diet includes frog eggs, lizard eggs, frogs and tadpoles. Between 8–13 eggs, measuring 18–22 x 27–33mm are produced at a time; hatchlings measure 210mm. Bornean records are from Brunei, Sarawak and Sabah and Kalimantan. Extralimital populations have been found in southern China, Thailand, the Malay Peninsula, Sumatra, the Mentawai Archipelago and Java.

Half-keeled Kukri Snake *Oligodon subcarinatus* 390mm

A poorly-known egg-eating snake. Head short, scarcely distinct from neck; eyes small, pupil rounded; midbody scale rows 17, with weak keels; ventrals 154–158; subcaudals 50–57; anal entire; dorsum reddish-brown, with 20–30 light cross-bars; a chevron pattern on forehead; venter orange-red. Inhabits lowland forests, between sea level to 200m, and has been found in buttresses of large trees. Its diet and reproductive habits are unknown. Known from Sarawak and Sabah, in Borneo, as well as the Malay Peninsula and Singapore.

Corrugated Water Snake *Opisthotropis typica* 490mm

A dark water snake, with shovel-like snout, from the plains and midhills of Borneo. Body slender; snout flattened; body scales with strong keels; forehead scales finely striated; eyes small, separated from labials by small scales; midbody scale rows 19; ventrals 160–176; subcaudals 82–96; dorsum unpatterned blackish-grey. Known to forage at night on banks of shallow, rocky streams, and associated with swamp pools and streams in the plains and midhills. It feeds on tadpoles. Reproductive biology unknown. Recorded from Brunei, Sarawak and Sabah, and is endemic to Borneo.

Mountain Reed Snake *Oreocalamus hanitschi* 570mm

A thick-set burrowing snake, from the mountainous regions of northern and north-western Borneo. Head and neck not differentiated; tail short, with a sharp tip; midbody scales 17, smooth; ventrals 125–132; subcaudals 21–32; dorsum brownish-tan, with dark brown scales arranged to form a zig-zag pattern; on the lower flanks, the dark scales join to form a continuous line; a dark stripe along eyes; a dark inverted chevron on neck; venter yellowish-brown, each ventral with black spots in the centre and on edges, that form a dark line. Associated with oak forests, at elevations of 1,120–1,525m, and feeds on earthworms. Its reproductive biology is unstudied. Known from the Kinabalu and Mendolong regions of Sabah and the Kelabit Plateau of Sarawak, this species has also been collected in the Malay Peninsula (Gunung Brinchang, at 1,700m).

Cave Racer *Orthriophis taeniurus* 2m

A cave-frequenting rat snake, that also occurs in lowland and submontane forests. A large-growing snake; midbody scales 25, smooth; ventrals 271–305; subcaudals 86–112; dorsum greyish-brown or greyish-black, a cream or tan stripe along middle of back, especially on the posterior; forehead olive; sides of head with a dark stripe; upper lips and chin cream; venter yellow or cream. Inhabits lowland forests, up to 2,000m, and often inhabits limestone caves, where bats roost. It feeds mostly on injured bats and swiftlets in such environments. Clutches of 11–13 are laid at a time. Known from Sarawak, Sabah and Kalimantan, this wide-ranging species is distributed from mainland South-east Asia to Sundaland.

Keeled Slug-eating Snake *Pareas carinatus* 600mm

A snail- and slug-eating snake. Head large; distinct from neck; a series of suboculars separate labials from the eye; pupil vertical; dorsal scales enlarged and keeled; midbody scale rows 15; ventrals 161–189; subcaudals 53–80; anal entire; dorsum brown, yellow or reddish-brown, with dark transverse bars; a dark streak along each eye; venter pale brown to yellow. Inhabits lowland forests, up to about 1,300m, on low vegetation; its diet comprises molluscs. Of its reproductive habits, nothing is known except that is is an egg-layer, producing up to eight eggs. Known from southern China, Myanmar, Thailand, Vietnam, Laos, Cambodia, the Malay Peninsula and Sumatra.

Painted Mock Viper *Psammodynastes pictus* 550mm

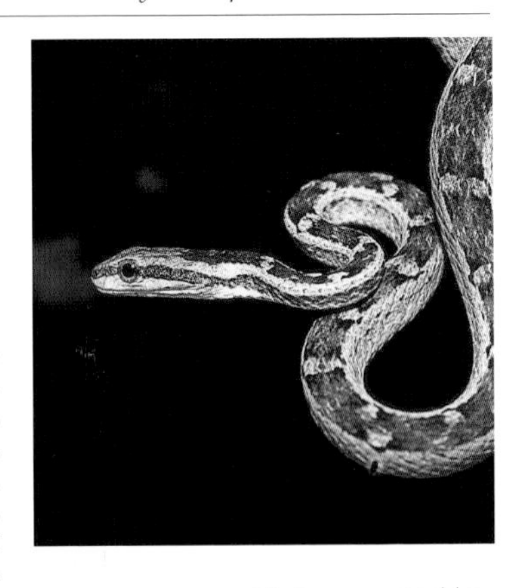

An ambush-feeding snake, associated with vegetation overhanging waterbodies. Head flattened, distinct from neck; third lower labial large and borders the mental groove; midbody scale rows 17; ventrals 152–171; subcaudals 60–80; dorsum brown or tan, sometimes black; dark-edged light transverse bands; a dark streak along eyes; venter cream, with brown speckles. Known from lowlands, its primary diet comprises fish, frogs, lizards and prawns. Reproductive habits unknown, except that it is ovoviviparous. Known from Sarawak and Sabah and Kalimantan, within Borneo. Also from the Malay Peninsula, Sumatra, the Riau and Mentawai Archipelagos.

Common Mock Viper *Psammodynastes pulverulentus* 55cm

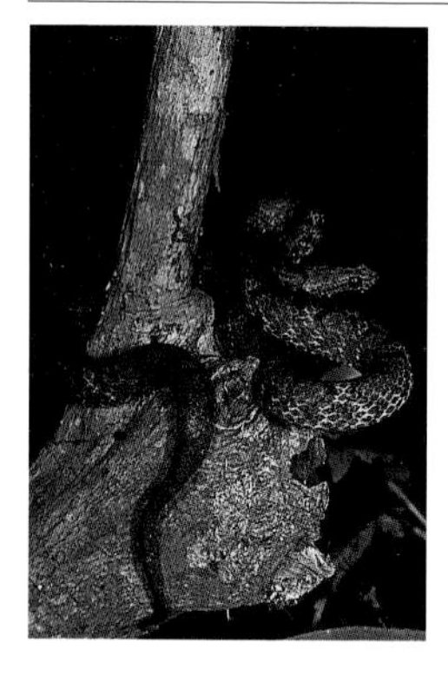

A feisty ground-dwelling or semi-arboreal snake, it is rather similar in morphology to a pit viper. Head flattened, distinct from neck; snout short; eyes large with vertical pupil; midbody scale rows 17 or 19, smooth; ventrals 146–175; subcaudals 44–70; dorsum colouration reddish-brown to yellowish-grey, or even black, with small dark spots or streaks; a longitudinal stripe along middorsal region and three longitudinal stripes along flanks, commencing from forehead; venter spotted with brown or grey and also dark spots or longitudinal lines. Inhabits lowland to midhills, and is terrestrial, but can climb low bushes. Active at dawn and at dusk, as well as at night; daytime activity also known. The teeth are modified for feeding on heavily-scaled vertebrates, such as skinks; frogs, geckos and the occasional small snake are also consumed. This snake bites readily, and is rear-fanged. Ovoviviparous, producing 3–10 young ones several times a year. Bornean records of this species are from Sarawak, Sabah and Kalimantan, the distribution in general extending from eastern India and Nepal, southern China, to mainland and insular south-east Asia, including the Philippines.

White-collared Reed Snake *Pseudorabdion albonuchalis* 196mm

A poorly-known leaf-litter dwelling snake. Head not distinct from neck; snout pointed; nostril between two shields; tail short; midbody scale rows 15, smooth; ventrals 127–144; anal entire; subcaudals 43–64; dorsum iridescent black or black; a broad yellow or red collar; venter dark brown. Inhabits lowland forests. Diet presumably includes small arthropods. Reproductive habits unknown. Recorded from Brunei, Sarawak and Sabah, but not from Kalimantan. Endemic to Borneo.

Dwarf Reed Snake *Pseudorabdion longiceps* 230mm

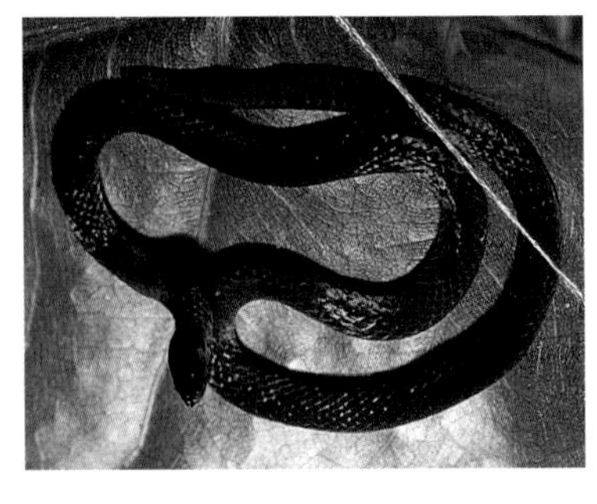

Another leaf litter dweller. Head not distinct from neck; snout pointed; nostril in a single shield; tail short, pointed; midbody scale rows 15, smooth; ventrals 129–147; anal entire; subcaudals 10–28; dorsum iridescent black or brown; a yellow collar and yellow spot above angle of mouth; venter dark brown. Inhabits lowland rainforests and, also, plantations and ricefields. It feeds on litter invertebrates, earthworms and small insects and their larvae. Three eggs are produced at a time. The distribution of the species includes Brunei, Kalimantan and Sarawak. Outside Borneo, this snake has been recorded from Thailand, the Malay Peninsula, Sumatra, the Mentawai and Riau Archipelagos and Sulawesi.

Keeled Rat Snake *Ptyas carinata* 3.8m

A very large rat snake, and perhaps the largest member of its family in Asia, it is sometimes mistaken for the King Cobra. Head distinct from neck; midbody scale rows 16 or 18; ventrals 208–215; subcaudals 110–118; anal divided; anterior of body olive-brown to nearly black, sometimes with indistinct yellow cross-bars; posterior of body yellow with a distinct black chequered pattern, terminating in a black tail with yellow spots; venter cream, turning grey or black posteriorly. Inhabits lowland forests and agricultural fields, it feeds on amphibians and rodents and is oviparous, laying 10 eggs at a time that take about 60 days to hatch. Bornean records of the species are from Brunei, Sarawak and Kalimantan, and the species has also been recorded from southern China, Myanmar, Thailand, the Malay Peninsula, Sumatra, Java and Palawan in the Philippines.

White-bellied Rat Snake *Ptyas fusca* 3m

Another large rat snake, also common in the lowlands. Head distinct from neck; midbody scale rows 16, smooth; ventrals 183–198; subcaudals 160–179; anal divided; dorsum brown with a red vertebral stripe. Little is known of its natural history, except that it is oviparous, and may feed on chickens, presumably raiding chicken runs. The species has a wide altitudinal distribution, from sea level to about 1,330m, in a variety of habitats – wet forests, scrubland and plantations, usually in the vicinity of water. Bornean records of the species are from Sarawak, Sabah and Kalimantan, and it has also been recorded from Sumatra, Nias and Peninsular Malaysia.

Javan Rat Snake *Ptyas korros* 2.2m

A large, terrestrial and also arboreal rat-eating snake. Head elongate, distinct from neck; eyes large; pupil rounded; midbody scales rows 15, smooth; ventrals 160–187; subcaudals 120–147; dorsum grey to olive-brown, the posterior of body darkening to nearly black; scales edged with white, becoming more distinct posteriorly, till they appear as white bands on a black background; venter and also chin and lips brownish-cream. Mostly terrestrial, but known to climb trees to rest and also to mate. Known from lowland forests, its diet includes rodents. Clutches comprise 4–12 eggs that are produced in June, and additional clutches may also be born. Incubation period is 61 days, hatchlings measuring 290mm. Bornean records of this species are from Kalimantan; extralimital populations range from eastern India and eastern China, to South-east Asia.

Speckle-bellied Keelback Snake *Rhabdophis chrysargos* 98cm

A large-eyed snake, with **toxic saliva**. Head distinct from neck; tail relatively short; eyes large; pupil rounded; midbody scale rows 19, keeled; ventrals 139–153; subcaudals 67–87; dorsum olive-grey; upper labials cream with darker smudges; a narrow cream chevron on neck, edged with black; a reddish-brown or orange band behind the neck; rest of back with yellow and brown, oblong marks, within darker bands; venter yellow with brown mottlings. The vertical distribution of this species ranges between 100–1,500m, and is associated with streams. Its diet includes frogs. Between 3–10 eggs, measuring 12–21 x 19.5–33.5mm, are produced at a time. After an incubation of 51–61 days, hatchlings measuring 148–220mm emerge. On Borneo, it has been recorded from Sabah and Sarawak as well as Kalimantan. Also reported from Myanmar, Thailand, Vietnam, Laos, Cambodia and the Malay Peninsula. From insular regions of South-east Asia, this species has been recorded from Sumatra, Java, Sulawesi, Bali, Flores, Nias, Simeulue, Ternate, as well as from the Philippines.

Red-bellied Keelback Snake *Rhabdophis conspicillata* 55cm

Another related lowland species. Head distinct from neck; tail short; midbody scale rows 19, keeled; ventrals 141–152; subcaudals 51–60; dorsum brown to reddish-brown; sides of head with a cream postocular stripe that curves downwards; upper lip cream; nape and neck with two narrow cream collars; venter yellow, each ventral scale with a dark edge. Distributed in lowland forests from 100–1,000m, generally in the vicinity of waterbodies, but sometimes also on the leaf litter, tree buttresses or under rotting logs and stones. Its diet and reproductive habits are unknown. Besides Borneo, where it has been found in Sarawak, Sabah and Kalimantan, this species is also found in the Malay Peninsula, Sumatra and the Natuna Archipelago.

Fire-lipped Keelback Snake *Rhabdophis murudensis* 873mm

A montane keelback snake, known from the high mountains of Sabah and Sarawak. Body robust; a single anterior temporal; three postoculars; midbody scale rows 19; ventrals 176–185; subcaudals 63–97; dorsum brownish-grey, with indistinct dark cross-bars; a row of light spots on the edges of the dark cross-bars; upper labials bright red; venter greyish-yellow, with small black spots. The elevational distribution of this species is between 915–2,500m, making it a lower- and upper montane forest species. Nuchal glands on the dorsal aspect of neck are present that presumably exude secretions to deter predators. Diet includes frogs. Reproductive habits remain unknown. Known localities include Gunung Murud and Gunung Mulu, both in Sarawak and Gunung Kinabalu and Trus Madi, in Sabah.

Bornean Black Snake *Stegonotus borneensis* 130cm

A dark-coloured, patternless snake from the low hills, up to submontane limits (1,750m) of Borneo. Head distinct from neck; distinct vertebral ridge present; pupil vertically elliptical; midbody scale rows 17, smooth; ventrals 194–233; subcaudals 60–79, paired; vertebral scales enlarged; dorsum grey-black, without lighter markings; supralabials grey with a pink tinge; each scale on venter alternatively banded with dark and light grey. Primarily terrestrial, it has been found both by day and by night. When threatened, it exudes a secretion with an unpleasant odour from its cloacal glands. Dietary habits unknown, and it is oviparous. Known localities include Kapit in central Sarawak and the submontane areas of Gunung Kinabalu, in Sabah, making it a Bornean endemic.

Stoliczka's Stream Snake *Stoliczkia borneensis* 750mm

A submontane and montane species, associated with stream banks. Body slender, laterally compressed, with a sharp ridge on the vertebral region; head wider than neck; nostrils large and flaring; eyes small and beady; midbody scale rows 33–35, keeled; ventrals 205–210; subcaudals 117–124; dorsum bluish-brown, with darker squarish marks; several dark bars behind head; venter unpatterned brown. It has also been found in low vegetation on stream banks, at night. Its diet and reproductive habits remain unknown. Besides Kinabalu and Trus Madi, in Sabah, it has been recorded from Gunung Murud, in Sarawak, the altitudinal range of the species between 800–1,800m. Endemic to Borneo.

Spotted Keelback Snake *Xenochrophis maculatus* 100cm

A slender, large-eyed water snake. Head distinct from neck; two anterior temporals; midbody scale rows 19, keeled; ventrals 140–156; subcaudals 95–117; anal divided; dorsum brownish-olive, with four longitudinal series of small dark squarish marks, and a paired row of yellow spots; head dark brown or black; upper lips yellow with darker smudges; venter yellow. Associated with low-lying areas, such as streams, ditches and other wetlands. Frogs and toads comprise its exclusive food, and its reproductive habits remain unknown. Within Borneo, known from Sarawak, Sabah and Kalimantan. Widely distributed in Peninsular Malaysia, Sumatra and the Natuna Archipelago.

Red-sided Keelback Snake *Xenochrophis trianguligerus* 135cm

A snake associated with wetlands, specializing in eating frogs, frog eggs and tadpoles. Head large, distinct from neck; tail short; midbody scale rows 19, keeled; ventrals 134–145; subcaudals 86–97; dorsum blackish-brown, with orangish-red triangles on sides of neck and front portion of body; these bright colours turn olive-brown or grey in older individuals; dark triangle-shaped marks on top of body; lips cream, some scales on lips black-edged; venter cream. Inhabits streams and standing water bodies in lowlands rainforests, as well as fields of rice paddies, roadside ditches and the vicinity of villages, ascending to1,350m. Diet comprises amphibians. Clutches of 5–15 eggs, measuring 15–17 x 29–34mm, are produced at a time. Bornean records of snake are from Brunei, Sarawak, Sabah and Kalimantan. Records outside of Borneo include Myanmar, Thailand, Vietnam, Sumatra, the Mentawai Archipelago, Java, Sulawesi, in Indonesia and the Nicobar Archipelago of India.

Rough-backed Litter Snake *Xenodermus javanicus* 650mm

A ground-dwelling snake with several strange features: three rows of large keeled scales on dorsum; nasal scales very large and flaring nostrils that point forward. Head rather large; ventrals 171–186; subcaudals 133–165; dorsum grey, unpatterned; venter cream, with black areas. Inhabits lowland forests in Borneo, although in Java, they are relatively common around agricultural areas, burrowing in the soft earth, up to an elevation of 1,100m. Its diet comprises frogs. Between 2–4 eggs are produced at a time. Besides Sabah and Sarawak, in Borneo, this strange snake has been reported from Myanmar, Thailand, Peninsular Malaysia, Sumatra and Java.

CROTALIDAE (PIT VIPERS)

Pit vipers represent the most specialized of the **venomous snakes**, capable of delivering their venom during a bite through enlarged fangs that are foldable and hollow, much like hypodermic needles. **Their venom is haemotoxic, affecting the blood cells**. Pit vipers have sensory pits on the snout, which act as thermal detectors for locating warm-bodied prey, such as rats and birds.

Kinabalu Brown Pit Viper *Garthius chaseni* 650mm

A montane pit viper, restricted to the submontane limits of Gunung Kinabalu. A thick-set species: head flattened; snout blunt; eyes separated from labials by two rows of scales; tail short; midbody scale rows 17 or 19, keeled; ventrals 131–143; subcaudals 20–30; dorsum dark or reddish-brown, with darker blotches in paired rows anteriorly, that join to form bands towards the posterior; venter yellow, with large areas of grey. Inhabits the forest floor of submontane forests; its diet and reproductive habits remain unknown. Recorded only from Kinabalu, in Sabah, between elevations 915–1,550m, this species is endemic to Borneo.

Sumatran Pit Viper *Parias sumatranus* 1.6m

A large green pit viper with enormous fangs (over 10mm in length), from the lowlands of Borneo. Body thick-set; tail prehensile; forehead scales smooth; midbody scales 21; ventrals 182–191; subcaudals 57–66; dorsum green with black cross-bars that become more distinct with growth; upper labials light blue; tail reddish-brown (brighter in juveniles); venter yellowish-green. Common in lowland forests, up to 800m, they are found on low vegetation. This is potentially a dangerous pit viper species, able to inject large quantities of venom and rather active at night. Their diet comprises small mammals, birds and frogs. Breeding habits unknown. Fatalities from its bite are known, and this species therefore needs to be treated as **dangerously venomous**. It is also known from southern Thailand, the Malay Peninsula, Sumatra and the Mentawai Archipelago.

Sabah Pit Viper *Popeia sabahi* 619mm

A green pit viper, endemic to the high mountains (1,000–1,150m) across Borneo. Head triangular and distinct from body; first supralabial distinct from nasal; scales on forehead smooth or weakly keeled; midbody scale rows 21, ventrals 147–157; subcaudals 59–76; keeled; dorsum green, lacking cross-bars or a postocular marking; a ventrolateral stripe, red or rusty-red in males, white or yellow in females; eyes red or orange in males and females, orange or yellowish-green in juveniles. Arboreal and probably nocturnal, it is found on low vegetation of shrubs and branches; its diet and reproductive biology remains unstudied. Records of this species are scattered, from Kinabalu-Crocker Range in Sabah, Gunung Gading and Gunung Penrissen in Sarawak and Gunung Semedoem in west Kalimantan.

Bornean Leaf-nosed Pit Viper *Trimeresurus borneensis* 83cm

A thick-bodied, essentially ground-dwelling pit viper. Head triangular; forehead scales smooth; body scales smooth or weakly keeled; midbody scale rows 21; ventrals 155–170; subcaudals 46–58; tail prehensile; colouration variable, ranging from mottled light brown, through medium brown with dark brown saddle-like pattern, to bright yellow, with darker mottling; an oblique pale stripe across head, up to neck. Inhabits lowland forests and midhills up to about 1,130m, encountered on the forest floor, in buttresses or edges of forest trails, although juveniles can climb low vegetation. Small mammals are consumed, and its reproductive habits remain unstudied. Known from Brunei, Sarawak, Sabah and Kalimantan, and extralimitally, from southern Thailand, the Malay Peninsula and Sumatra.

A familiar arboreal pit viper measuring 96.3cm in length. Body slender in juveniles, relatively thick in adults; tail prehensile; Supralabial III separated from subocular by 1–2 scales; occipital scales distinctly keeled in males; 4–7 scales on snout of males, 5–8 in females; internasals separated by 2 (rarely 1) scales; midbody scale rows 21–23 in males, 21–29 in females; ventrals 127–148; subcaudals 40–54. Dorsum green or greenish-blue with blue, white and red spots or stripes in males; dorsum green or bluish-green with blue and red cross-bars in females; cream or yellow area below dark postocular stripe in adult females, white and red stripe in juveniles and males; venter uniform or blotched or spotted with blue or red. Inhabits lowland forests. Arboreal and associated with low vegetation as well as trees. Diet comprises birds and rodents. Ovoviviparous. Borneo, Also, many small island groups of western Indonesia and the Philippines.

CYLINDROPHIIDAE (PIPE SNAKES)

A family of fossorial snakes that are otherwise inoffensive, but are known to hunt and feed on snakes and eels. They are associated with low-lying, swampy areas, and have cylindrical bodies that can be flattened.

Red-tailed Pipe Snake *Cylindrophis ruffus* 900mm

A short-headed, burrowing snake; head blunt and indistinct from neck; eyes reduced; smooth scales, numbering 19–21 at midbody; tail short, bearing just 5–6 subcaudals; dorsum black, typically with a pale collar; bright orange on the body; venter with black cross-bars. Inhabits low, swampy habitats. Pipe snakes are specialized snake-eaters, and are known to swallow both venomous and non-venomous species. Eels are also eaten. When threatened, it raises its tail and waves it, perhaps to deflect attack by a predator to its posterior, rather than to its more vulnerable head. Ovoviviparous, producing 5–13 young, measuring 205mm. Known from Brunei and Sarawak, within Borneo, and extralimitally, from Myanmar, Thailand, southern China, Cambodia, Vietnam, the Malay Peninsula, Sumatra and associated islands, besides Sulawesi and Java.

ELAPIDAE (COBRAS, CORAL SNAKES AND KRAITS)

Cobras, coral snakes and kraits represent a family of **extremely venomous** snakes that have fixed fangs and produce neurotoxic venom whose **bite causes respiratory failure**. Borneo has several endemic species within this family. Cobras are primarily rat eaters, while kraits and coral snakes may feed on other snakes.

Banded Krait *Bungarus fasciatus* 225cm

A distinct banded snake, its yellow and black pattern cannot be mistaken for any other species. It differs from Mangrove Cat Snake (*Boiga dendrophila*) in showing dark bands that are nearly as broad as pale ones (as opposed to much narrower yellow bands). Body elongated, triangular in cross-section, with a raised vertebral region; tail short and stumpy, subcaudal scales undivided; midbody scale rows 15; ventrals 213–234; subcaudals 28–37; dorsum with alternating black and yellow bands that are approximately equal in size; and top of head with a V-shaped marking. Inhabits lowland areas, such as lightly forested areas and swamps. Although timid and non-aggressive by day, when it prefers to hide its head under its coils, it is known to be more active by night and **human deaths from its bite have occurred**. A snake-eating species, it is known to eat water snakes, rat snakes, pythons and vine snakes, although lizards, frogs, fishes and vertebrate eggs are also eaten. Clutches comprise 4–14 eggs that hatch after 61 days. Hatchlings measure 250–300mm. Known from Brunei, Sarawak, Sabah and Kalimantan, in Borneo, and extralimitally, India, Nepal, Bangladesh, Myanmar, China, Cambodia, Laos, Vietnam, Thailand, the Malay Peninsula, Sumatra and Java.

Red-headed Krait *Bungarus flaviceps* 1955cm

A large and **dangerously venomous** snake from the lowlands and mountains. Head large and snout blunt; tail relatively short; midbody scale rows 13, smooth; ventrals 206–225; subcaudals 42–52; dorsum blue-black with a yellow or tan vertebral stripe; red or yellow head and tail; venter pink or yellow. Associated with lowland and submontane forests, and diet comprises other snakes and lizards. The population from Gunung Kinabalu and Trus Madi (subspecies *baluensis*), between 200–750m, may be specifically distinct. A **dangerously venomous** snake, it attempts to bite when threatened, especially at night; most individuals try to conceal their heads under the coils of their bodies by day. Known from Sabah, Sarawak and Kalimantan, the range of this species includes Myanmar, Thailand, the Malay Peninsula, Vietnam and Sumatra.

Blue Coral Snake *Calliophis bivirgata* 185cm

A large and colourful **venomous** snake, that hides its head under its body, and prefers to expose its brightly coloured tail instead. Body slender; head short, not wider than neck; tail short, terminating in a sharp point; midbody scale rows 13, smooth; ventrals 243–304; subcaudals 37–49; dorsum dark blue to blue-black, with a distinct pale blue stripe along each side; head, tail and venter coral-red. An inhabitant of lowland forests, it may also be found in forest fringes, such as in agricultural areas. Its diet includes other snakes. Females lay 1–3 eggs of dimensions 35–35 x 9mm. **Extremely venomous**, there is no effective antivenom for its bite. Recorded from Brunei, Sarawak, Sabah and Kalimantan, the range of the species including Myanmar, Thailand, Cambodia, the Malay Peninsula, Sumatra and the Mentawai Archipelago.

Malayan Striped Coral Snake *Calliophis intestinalis* 71cm

A small but **deadly** species of elapid. Body slender; head small, not wider than neck; midbody scale rows 13, smooth; ventrals 206–240; subcaudals 21–26; dorsum reddish-brown to dark brown, a lighter stripe on the sides; some individuals with a red stripe; venter yellow, cream or red. Inhabits lowland forests, and may enter human-modified habitats, such as parks and gardens. A semi-fossorial snake that conceals under leaves, and feeds on other snakes. When threatened, it is known to raise its tail to expose its red underside, or even turn over backward, revealing its bright belly colours. Bornean records of the species are from Brunei, Sarawak, Sabah and Kalimantan. The range of the species extends from Thailand, the Malay Peninsula, to Sumatra, the Mentawai Archipelago, Java and Sulawesi. Although small, it should be treated with caution, and **human fatalities from its bite are known**.

Sumatran Cobra *Naja sumatrana* 150cm

Above: juvenile; below: adult

A true spitting cobra, this species can spray a fine jet of venom up to a distance of nearly 1m, so appropriate **precaution should be taken when in proximity of this species**. Head large, snout rounded; hood rounded in adults, more elongate in juveniles; midbody scale rows 17–19; ventrals 187–206; subcaudals 42–53; dorsum metallic blue-black; hood without markings in adults; juvenile with yellow-cream bands. Known from lightly forested areas and enters human dwellings around towns and villages. Diet includes rodents and other small vertebrates. Known from Brunei, Sarawak, Sabah and Kalimantan, and outside of Borneo, it has been recorded from southern Peninsular Thailand, the Malay Peninsula, Sumatra, Palawan in the southern Philippines. Systematic comparisons between these populations are required.

King Cobra *Ophiophagus hannah* 5.65m (2.62m for Borneo)

The largest and arguably most dramatic snake on earth is the King Cobra. It differs from all other snakes in showing a paired postoccipital. In addition, the head is large. Scalation data for Bornean populations include: ventrals 254–264 and subcaudals 89–125; adults show 60–74 bands on body; dorsum brownish-black, nearly unpatterned in adults, scales on posterior and on tail slightly lighter in the centre; chin and throat yellow, rest of venter dark grey; juveniles with pale yellow or orange bands. Terrestrial in habits, it feeds exclusively on other snakes and occasionally, on monitor lizards. Females construct a mound nest by collecting fallen leaves with the aid of their bodies and tails, in which eggs are deposited and guarded. Clutches comprise 24 eggs and the incubation period is 63 days. Hatchlings measure 288–422mm. There are **a few authenticated cases of attacks by this species on humans**. Bornean records are from Brunei, Sarawak, Sabah and Kalimantan. Systematic studies on these snakes now in progress, suggest that several species are popularly referred to as being King Cobra. The distribution of these snakes range from eastern Pakistan, through India and other countries of southern Asia, southern and eastern China, Indo-China and Indo-Malaya, to the islands of the Philippines.

HYDROPHIIDAE (SEA SNAKES)

Sea snakes can be easily differentiated from all other families of snakes, even when they enter saltwater – they have flattened, paddle-like tails and short fangs at the back of their upper jaws. Sea snakes are completely aquatic and produce live young, never coming ashore, with the exception of the sea kraits, which bask, rest and lay eggs on small islands. Although mostly marine, some travel upriver, in tidal portions of rivers. They have fixed fangs, like cobras and kraits, and their bite is **extremely venomous**, although, due to the generally inaccessible nature of their habitats and their usually non-aggressive nature, few people are bitten.

Beaded Sea Snake *Aipysurus eydouxii* 100cm

This is a specialized fish-egg eating sea snake. Consequently, it has a 50- to 100-fold decrease in venom toxicity, compared to related species. A small sea snake; head shields symmetrical; supralabials not divided horizontally; pupil rounded; midbody scale rows 17, smooth; ventrals distinct throughout, numbering 141–149; subcaudals 27–30; forehead dark brown; dorsum with tan or yellowish-cream, dark-edged bands. Associated with shallow coastal waters. Its reproductive biology is unknown. The venom gland in this species is much reduced, as are the fangs. Known from the waters off Sabah, this species is distributed from Thailand, the Malay Peninsula, through the Sundas, to New Guinea, Australia and New Caledonia.

Hook-nosed Sea Snake *Enhydrina schistosa* 158cm

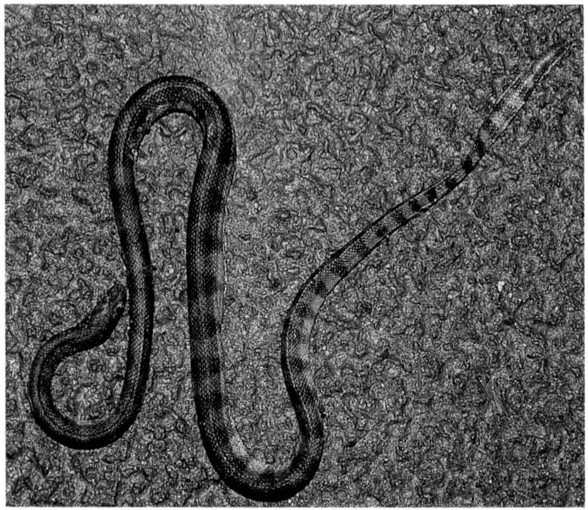

An unpredictable, **sometimes aggressive sea snake**, that is **responsible for a number of human casualties**. Scales are distinctly keeled; rostral scale on the upper jaw gives it a beak-like appearance; mental shields elongated; midbody scale rows 49–66; ventrals small, numbering 239–322; dorsum of body and forehead greyish-olive, the latter a little darker, body with indistinct darker markings; venter cream in front, darkening to greenish-yellow towards the tail. Commonly found on sea-coasts and in mangroves, it is a specialist predator of marine catfishes, and is frequently taken in fishing nets and killed in large numbers. Ovoviviparous, gravid females known between December and February, and clutches are 4–11, the newborns measuring 254–280mm in length. Known from isolated localities, especially on the north-west coast of Borneo, the range of this species extends from the Persian Gulf, through southern Asia, east to New Guinea and northern Australia.

Annulated Sea Snake *Hydrophis cyanocinctus* 188.5cm

A small sea snake, with strongly keeled scales. Head small, almost indistinct from neck, the body thickening towards the posterior; midbody scale rows 37–47; ventrals 292–389; colour and pattern variable: dorsum typically olive or yellow, with bluish-black transverse bands that may or may not encircle the body; venter yellowish-cream. Found in shallow coastal waters and are often captured by prawn trawls. The diet of this species includes fishes, especially gobies and eels, and also marine invertebrates. Ovoviviparous, 3–16 young ones, measuring 381mm, are born at a time. Widespread in coastal areas, from the Persian Gulf, east including South-east Asia and Japan.

Sibau River Sea Snake *Hydrophis sibauensis* 650mm

A recently described member of an essentially marine family of snakes, this species was collected over 1,000km upriver. A medium-sized snake, its head is much slenderer than the body; nostril situated on top of head; forehead shields large and regular; dorsal scales with median keel; ventrals small and distinct throughout; ventrals 257–264; midbody scale rows 35–37; forehead black with small yellow spots and arrow-shaped markings; body grey-brown, darkening posteriorly; 49–58 yellow to light orange bands on body; venter black anteriorly, greyish-yellow from midbody to posterior of body. Inhabits the Sibau River, which shows fluctuations in width between the dry and wet seasons, of about 60–85m, and depth of about 2–17m. Diet unknown, and seven live young are produced at a time. Known only from River Sibau, a branch of the Kapuas River, in Kalimantan, western Borneo.

Annandale's Sea Snake *Kolpophis annandalei* 520mm

An unmistakable species of sea snake, with a large number (74–93) of midbody scale rows of smooth or weakly keeled scales. Head narrower than widest part of body; fragmented head scales; ventrals 320–368; dorsum grey-blue with dark bands; venter pale yellow or cream; tail flattened. This poorly known species is known from isolated localities in South-east Asia. It is associated with a fish-eating diet and sandy-bottom coast. The only specimen obtained in Borneo was caught by a fisherman in shallow waters, using hook and line, baited with fish, at Brunei's Tungku Beach, near Bandar Seri Begawan. The species is otherwise known from the Malay Peninsula, Thailand, Vietnam, and possibly Sumatra, from the sea-coasts as well as freshwater environments.

Short Sea Snake *Lapemis curtus* 972mm

A stout-bodied sea snake with a relatively large head that is broad and short; scales squarish or hexagonal, the lowermost rows especially in males with a short keel, giving it a thorn-like appearance; midbody scale rows 25–43; ventrals 114–274; dorsum brownish-grey to olive, with lighter bands, that taper on the sides; venter unpatterned yellow or cream. Females are larger and heavier than males, and in addition, have smooth scales, while males have keeled scales. Inhabits seas with muddy bottoms and diet comprises fishes, especially eels, gobies and catfishes, although squid and other marine invertebrates are also eaten. Between 1–6 young ones are produced at a time, measuring 373mm. The distribution of this marine snake is from the Persian Gulf to South-east Asia, and on the west coast of Sabah. This is the most common sea snake caught by trawlers.

Yellow-lipped Sea Krait *Laticauda colubrina* 171cm

A partially-terrestrial, egg-laying sea snake, often encountered on rocky islands off the coast. A large species; ventrals 213–245, broad; midbody scale rows 21–25, smooth; subcaudals 29–47; a dark-light banded species, black annuli numbering 36–50, and are separated by bluish-grey bands. Adult males are much smaller than females. This is the commonest sea snake locally, abundant in rocky islands off the coast. A non-aggressive species, it rarely bites, but has a **highly toxic venom**, and deaths from its bite are documented. It comes ashore, to lay eggs, bask, rest and perhaps also to digest food. Diet comprises eels. Clutches of 3–13 eggs, measuring 44.6–92.2 x 20.3–31.1mm are produced in caves of rocky islands. This species has a wide distribution in the Indian and Pacific Oceans, from India and Sri Lanka, east to Polynesia and other areas of the Pacific Ocean. Within Borneo, records of the species are from Brunei, Sarawak and Sabah.

Pelagic Sea Snake *Pelamis platura* 100cm

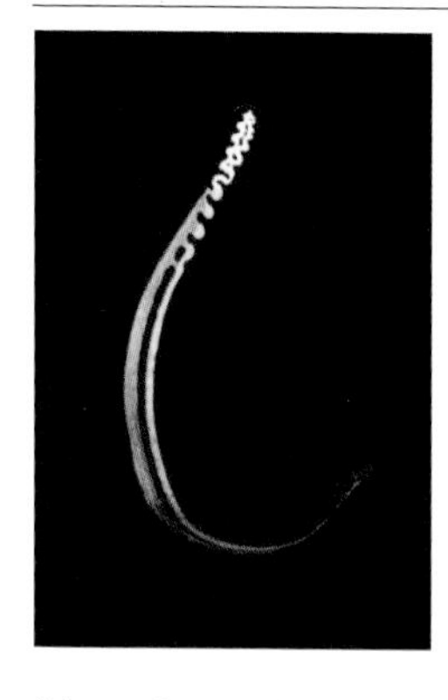

A sea snake from the open ocean, as well as from sea-coasts, this is the most widespread species of snake in the world. Head rather elongated and slightly flattened, distinct from the slender neck; body greatly compressed; ventrals 264–406, irregular in shape and indistinct after the front portion of the body; dorsum black or dark brown; venter light brown or yellow; tail with a bright yellow diamond-shaped pattern. Aggressive, unlike most other sea snakes, with a **highly toxic venom**. Barnacles are often found encrusting its skin. Diet comprises fish, and most feeding occurs on the surface or close to the surface. Recorded occasionally from the coasts of Borneo. The enormous distribution of the species includes the eastern part of the Pacific Ocean and the snake also occurs in cold temperate waters.

TYPHLOPIDAE (BLIND SNAKES)

Worm-like in external appearance, blind snakes are burrowers, living under the soil and in the leaf litter. They frequently appear on land during the rains, when they are flooded out of their subterranean haunts. Worms, ants, termites and their larvae form their dietary mainstay.

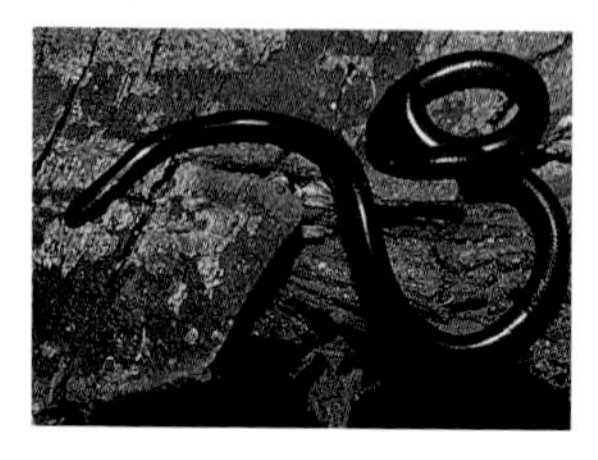

Common Blind Snake
Ramphotyphlops braminus
180mm

A small, dark, worm-like snake, with a rounded head, nostrils placed laterally; eyes distinct; four supralabials; head scales larger than body scales; tail ends in a spine; 20 midbody scale rows, diameter of body 30–45 times total length; transverse rows of scales ranging between 290–320; dorsally, black or brown, ventrally lighter; snout and tip of tail are paler in colouration. Encountered on the soil during heavy rains. It has also been recorded on trees, perhaps while it hunts for termites and ants, which almost exclusively comprise its food. This snake has been introduced throughout the world by humans, in flowerpots, and is an all-female species, producing eggs without mating. It occurs all over tropical and subtropical regions of Asia, as well as Central and North America, Australia, Africa and islands in Indian and Pacific Oceans. Within Borneo, it has been recorded from Brunei, Sabah and Sarawak, but curiously, not from Kalimantan, almost certainly due to limited work conducted there.

Müller Blind Snake *Typhlops muelleri* 480mm

A burrowing snake, recorded from Borneo without a precise locality. Head short, blunt; eyes reduced; rostral broad and short, being half the head width; midbody scale rows 26 or 28; a spine-like projection at the end of tail; dorsum dark brown or grey-black and venter yellow or cream. Lives in soft soil, and also, under rocks and logs in lowland forests. Diet includes the larvae of ants and termites, although molluscs and other snakes have also been reported. Ovoviviparous, between 5–14 young ones are born at a time. Known from Borneo, Sumatra and Peninsular Malaysia.

Olive Blind Snake *Ramphotyphlops olivaceus* 430mm

A burrowing species like others in the family. Body slender; snout projecting with narrow transverse edge; rostral large, over half head width; nasal incompletely divided; preocular present; eye distinct; midbody scale rows 20–22; total length 40–85 times midbody diameter; caudal spine present. Dorsum pale brown; venter paler. Probably oviparous, clutch size 3. Known from Borneo (Sarawak), and also, Sangihe, Seram and Mysool (Indonesia) and Samar and Babuan (the Philippines).

XENOPELTIDAE (SUNBEAM SNAKES)

The two living species of this family look like living holograms, with very smooth, iridescent dorsal scales. In addition, they show short tails and rather cylindrical bodies. They are burrowers, with a flattened snout, and feed on warm-bodied prey, such as rats. A second species is known from eastern China.

Sunbeam Snake *Xenopeltis unicolor* 114cm

Head hardly distinct from body, depressed; snout rounded; eyes small with vertically elliptical pupil; nostrils situated between two nasals; a large interparietal in middle of four parietals; mental groove present; fourth and fifth supralabials entering eye; a small supraocular; midbody scale rows 15; ventrals 164–196, enlarged; subcaudals 24–31; anals divided; tail short. Dorsally, iridescent brown, each scale light-edged; juveniles with a cream collar; venter white or cream. In juveniles, a pale yellow collar is typically present. In Borneo, this species is known from lowland sites, generally close to the coast, and is known to enter human habitations. It feeds on rodents and frogs. Clutches of three eggs are produced, measuring 18 x 58mm. On Borneo, this species is known from Brunei, Sabah, Sarawak and Kalimantan. Widespread in Indo-Malayan region, it has been recorded from Myanmar and south-eastern China, south to Thailand, the Nicobar Archipelago of India, Indo-China, the Philippines and the Malay Peninsula and Archipelago.

Agamas or 'Dragons' are day-active lizards, usually with a crest on head and body (especially in adult males), and have well-developed limbs and tail. Most species live on trees and bushes in forested areas; there are some that dwell on sand or on rocks. Nearly all are insectivorous, sitting in wait for appropriate-sized insects and or invertebrates to come within striking distance. A few supplement their diet by eating flower petals and seeds. They dig shallow nests on the earth, in which their soft-shelled eggs are deposited. Perhaps the most remarkable members are the flying lizards (*Draco*), which have evolved elongated ribs covered with skin, that permit them to make spectacular glides between trees.

Long-snouted Shrub Lizard *Aphaniotis acutirostris* 72mm

A long-snouted lizard from western Borneo. Body slender, compressed; snout acute, much longer than eye diameter; a projecting convex scale above rostral; limbs long; dorsal scales small, with scattered larger scales; a row of tuberculate scales on paravertebral region; dewlap weak; males with a weak nuchal crest; preanal and femoral pores absent; ventral scales keeled; dorsal surface brown with darker variegation; dark radiating lines from orbit of eye; throat sometimes with dark spots; rest of ventral surface pale brown; males with a distinct yellow dewlap; and inner lining of mouth blue. Inhabits lowland rainforests, and found on shrub-like vegetation. Diet presumably comprises small insects and other invertebrates. Two eggs are laid every 30–100 days, measuring 7 x 12mm, hatching 48–63 days later. Known from western Kalimantan, and also Sumatra and adjacent islands.

Brown Shrub Lizard *Aphaniotis fusca* 67mm

A slender lizard from lowland forests and midhills. Body slender, compressed; snout rounded, not longer than diameter of eye; limbs long; fifth toe longer than first; dorsal scales small, with scattered larger scales; nuchal crest reduced, composed of short triangular scales; dewlap weak, especially in females; tail long, slender, ending in a blunt tip; dorsum dark brown or brownish-olive; venter pale olive-brown; two dark interorbital bars; inner lining of mouth dark blue, especially in adult males; gular sac in adult males black with oval yellow spots; dorsal surface of tail with indistinct dark bands; dorsal surface of limbs unbarred; and undersurfaces of limbs and tail pale brown. Inhabits primary and lightly disturbed lowland forests and midhills, including dipterocarp forests; diurnal and arboreal, feeding on caterpillars, beetles, millipedes, cockroaches and termites. Clutches of 1–2 eggs of dimensions 7 x 18mm, are produced; hatchlings measure 23–43mm. Known from Sarawak, and possibly also Sabah and Kalimantan, this species is distributed from southern Thailand, the Malay Peninsula, Sumatra, Simalur, Nias, Borneo, Singkep and the Natuna Islands.

Ornate Shrub Lizard *Aphaniotis ornata* 57mm

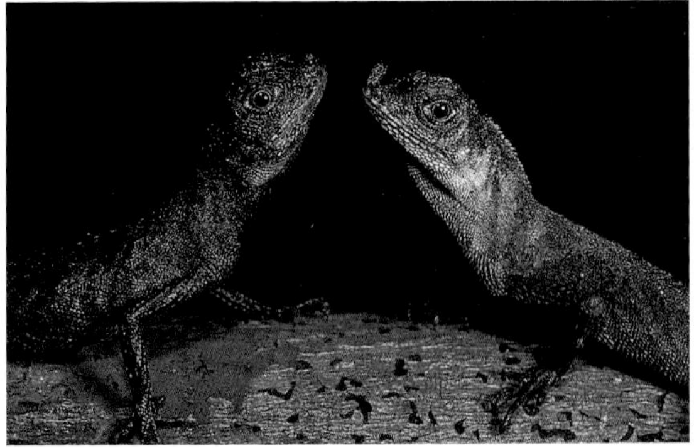

A shrub lizard with a rostral appendage. Body slender, compressed; snout as long as eye diameter; snout-tip with a fleshy conical appendage that points backwards, narrowest at base and covered with keeled scales; tympanum not exposed; supralabials 8–9; infra-labials 8–9, both keeled; males with a low nuchal crest comprising erect scales; limbs long; dorsal scales small, with scattered larger scales; forehead scales keeled; dewlap and fold weak; preanal and femoral pores absent; dorsal surface medium brown to brownish-red; small yellow spot on each side of eyelids; rostral appendage brown; lining of mouth pale blue; gular sac yellow-cream; venter yellowish-cream; and tail banded with yellow, more distinct apically. Inhabits lowland rainforests and midhills of Sabah, eastern Kalimantan and Brunei, up to an elevation of about 900m. Encountered on saplings and tree trunks, and is diurnal and insectivorous. Two eggs, measuring 7 x 15mm, are produced.

Crested Green Lizard *Bronchocela cristatella* 130mm

A familiar green tree lizard from parks and gardens of Bornean towns and cities, as well as lowland forests and the lower montane forests. Body slender, compressed; head long; nuchal crest weak, with elongate scales; dorsal crest somewhat distinct, middorsal scale rows 60–100; lamellae under toe IV 34–35; dorsal surface bright green, sometimes with white or light blue spots that may form bars, or with white bars, changeable to brown, with indistinct dark bands on body and tail, when threatened; a pale grey stripe across the eyes; tympanum brown; and venter yellowish-green. Widespread in the lowlands and midhills, up to about 1,700m. Diurnal and arboreal, it is capable of making short glides, and is found on shrubs, tree trunks as well as fences and walls. Diet includes mayflies, beetles, flies and ants, in addition to skinks. Eggs are spindle-shaped, with pointed ends, measuring 30–35.8 x 8.1–11mm and 1–4 eggs are produced per clutch. Within Borneo, it is widespread in suitable habitats within its elevational range. Distributed from southern Myanmar, Thailand, the Nicobar Archipelago, the Malay Peninsula, Sumatra, Borneo, Java, the Lesser Sundas, Makulu and the Philippines.

Maned Forest Lizard *Bronchocela jubata* 150mm

A rather rare (in Borneo) tree lizard from Kalimantan; body relatively robust; nuchal and dorsal crest with elongated scales; limbs relatively long; nuchal and dorsal crest comprising lanceolate scales that point posteriorly; supralabials 9–10; infralabials 8–9; midbody scale rows 43–53; a row of large scales along chin, parallel to labials; ventral scales large, strongly keeled; dewlap reaches pectoral region; dorsum green, changeable to brown or black, with yellow or red spots or vertical bars. Inhabits lowland forests as well as disturbed areas. Diet comprises insects, and two eggs, measuring 44–53 x 9.5–12mm are produced at a time, although more than one clutch may be produced in a year. Hatchlings measure 162mm. Known from Kalimantan, within Borneo, as well as Java, Bali, Singkep, Sulawesi, Karakelang and Salibabu Archipelagos.

Horned Flying Lizard *Draco cornutus* 88.9mm

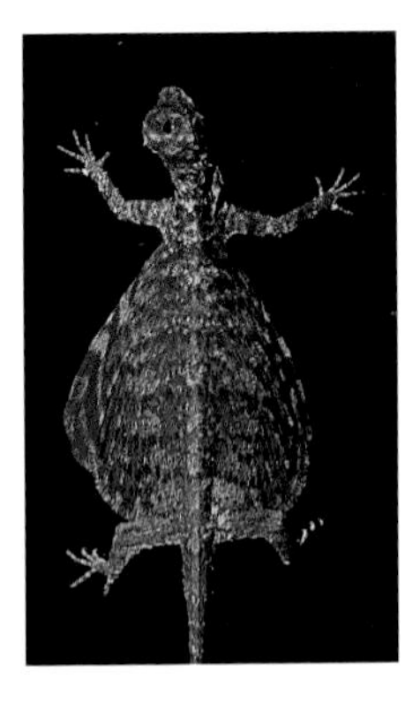

A brightly-coloured flying lizard from primary forests, including mangrove swamps. Body slender, with a thorn-like scale over eye that is over 0.6mm; tympanum scaleless; dewlap triangular, covered with small scales; nostrils oriented laterally; dorsal crest absent; neck lappets with large scales; males and females with a reduced nuchal crest consisting of triangular scales; supralabials 8–10; lamellae under toe IV 20–27; dorsals smooth, sometimes intermixed with some larger scales; dorsum bright green to greenish-brown, in males; tan or light brown in females; patagium reddish-orange with dark spots or bands; a dark interorbital spot. Inhabits the plains and midhills, and feeds exclusively on small black ants. Gravid females have been found in July, and clutches of 3–4 are known. Occurs in Brunei, Sabah and Sarawak, in addition to Sumatra, Java, Bangunan Islands and the Sulu Archipelago.

Fringed Flying Lizard *Draco fimbriatus* 132mm

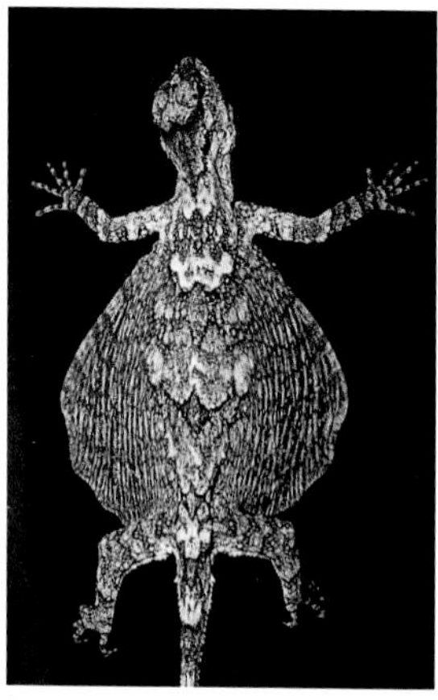

A gigantic flying lizard from primary forests. Body relatively robust; spinous projection over eye; tympanum large, scaleless; five patagial ribs; males with a low nuchal sail; nostrils oriented laterally; dewlap triangular, with small scales; supralabials 11; infralabials 9–12; males with a low nuchal sail and caudal crest comprising small triangular scales; posterior of thighs and tail-base with fringe-like scales; dorsum and patagium greyish-brown, with grey and pale green markings. Inhabits lowlands and midelevation forests, on trees as tall as 20m. Diet unknown and presumably comprises arthropods. A clutch of 2–4 eggs is laid at a time, measuring 16–17 x 10–11mm, and hatching takes place 40 days later. Known from Sarawak, Sabah and Kalimantan, its distribution includes southern Thailand, the Malay Peninsula, Sumatra, the Mentawai Archipelago, Borneo, Java and Mindanao in the Philippines.

Blood-bearded Flying Lizard *Draco haematopogon* 94mm

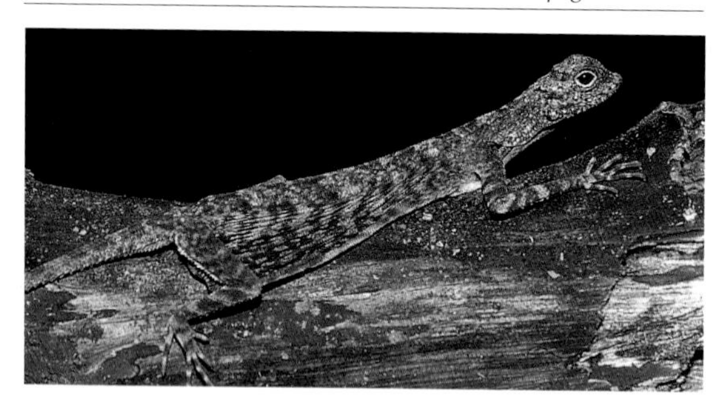

A slender flying lizard from montane forests. Body slender; tail crest absent; tympanum large, skin-covered; a row of keeled scales on snout; dewlap covered with small scales; no thorn-like scale above eyes; patagial ribs five; caudal crest absent; nostrils oriented dorsally; supralabials 11–12; subcaudals 1.2–1.6 times length of adjacent scales; dorsals 148–184; dorsum olive or brownish-grey, with indistinct lighter and darker spots; patagium black with yellow spots. Inhabits midhills and submontane forests, and diet probably comprises ants and other small insects. Between 2–3 eggs are produced at a time. Known from Sarawak, Sabah and Kalimantan, its range includes the Malay Peninsula, Sumatra, Java and Borneo.

Large Flying Lizard *Draco maximus* 139mm

A large, robust flying lizard. Body relatively robust; patagial ribs six; no spinous projection above eye; males with nuchal sail; dewlap covered with small scales; supralabials 14–15; dorsals mostly homogenous, with a small series of large scales at base of patagium; fringe-like scales on posterior margin of thighs and tail base; ventrals larger than dorsals, keeled; subcaudals 1.3–2 times larger than adjacent scales; dorsum green, with a brownish-olive pattern of bands; patagium black with discontinuous olive-brown lines. Inhabits river-edges from the lowlands to about 1,000m, and known to sleep on tree trunks, 1.5–2 m above ground. Its diet presumably comprises ants and other insects. Between 1–5 eggs, measuring 11 x 18mm, are produced at a time. Reported from Sarawak, Sabah and Kalimantan, and generally distributed in the Malay Peninsula, Sumatra, Borneo and the Natuna Islands.

Black-bearded Flying Lizard *Draco melanopogon* 93mm

A commonly-encountered flying lizard from non-riparian sections of the forest. Body slender; spinous projections above eye absent; dewlap elongate, scales covering dewlap slightly enlarged; patagial ribs five; nostrils oriented upwards; supralabials 12–13; dorsals smooth or weakly keeled, heterogeneous; a lateral row of large scales present; fringe-like scales on posterior of thighs and tail base; ventrals keeled, larger than dorsals; subcaudals 1.3–2 times larger than adjacent scales; dorsum olive or green with brownish-grey bands or diamond-shaped spots; patagium black with scattered yellow-orange spots, Inhabits lowland forests. Diet primarily comprises ants, although appropriately-sized beetles, millipedes, isopods and termites may also be consumed. Two eggs, measuring 6.5–7.6 x 14–15.7mm, and with rather pointed ends, are produced at a time. Known from Brunei, Sarawak, Sabah and Kalimantan, this species is widespread in South-east Asia, from Peninsular Thailand, the Malay Peninsula, Sumatra, Borneo and the Natuna Islands.

Five-banded Flying Lizard *Draco quinquefasciatus* 110mm

Perhaps the most common Bornean species of flying lizard within forested areas. Body slender; spinous projections on supraciliary absent; patagial ribs six; nostril oriented upwards; supralabials 12–14; dorsals heterogenous, mostly smooth; a lateral row of enlarged scales; posterior margin of thighs and tail-base with fringe-like scales; ventrals subequal to dorsals, keeled; subcaudals 1.3–2 times length of adjacent scales; dewlap tapering to a narrow tip; males with a low nuchal sail; dorsum bright green in males, brownish-olive in females, with dark specklings; patagium yellow or orangish-red above, with five dark brown or black cross-bars. Inhabits forests from the lowlands to the midhills, including peat swamps. Feeds exclusively on ants. Between 1–4 eggs, measuring 16.8–17.2 x 9.6–10.2mm, are produced. Hatchlings measure 30.3–30.4mm. Known from Brunei, Sarawak, Sabah and Kalimantan. This is essentially a Sundaic species, with a distribution from southern Thailand, the Malay Peninsula, Sumatra, Pulau Sinkep, Pulau Belitung and Borneo.

Common Flying Lizard *Draco sumatranus* 85mm

The commonest Bornean flying lizard, it is the most likely to be seen by the average city dweller. Body slender; tail crest absent; patagium with six (rarely five or seven) ribs; caudal crest absent; nostrils oriented laterally; dewlap triangular, covered with small scales; nuchal crest present, comprising 6–20 compressed, triangular or keeled scales in males, and up to 14 in females; supralabials 6–12; dorsals 103–166; males with blue forehead when displaying; dorsum light brown, with dark brown blotches; dewlap bright yellow, with black dots at base. Inhabits open forests, plantations, parks and gardens, in the lowlands (up to about 300m). Often observed basking and displaying during midday, the home ranges of adult males are 1–3 adjacent trees, and glides are more commonly seen in the more active males, than in females. Diet includes ants, beetles and termites. Between 1–5 rounded eggs are produced at a time, between May–August and November–December. This familiar South-east Asian lizard has a wide distribution: Thailand, the Malay Peninsula, Sumatra, the Mentawai and Riau Archipelagos, Borneo and Palawan, and is known from all parts of Borneo within its elevational range.

Bornean Angle-headed Lizard *Gonocephalus bornensis* 136mm

A robust arboreal lizard, known from primary forests throughout Borneo. Body relatively robust; nuchal and dorsal crests continuous, highly developed in males, comprising elongated, lanceolate scales that run up to the level of the tail and decreasing in height posteriorly; females with a high nuchal crest but a lower dorsal crest; dorsal crest fused in juvenile males; dorsals intermixed with larger scales; no large scales below orbit of eye; ventrals smooth, more convex on the pectoral region; dorsum bright green with five dark bands; sides of head and flanks green-spotted; sides of body with light oval spots; nuchal and body crest brown and yellow; dewlap pale with dark, broken stripes. Inhabits primary rainforests in the midhills, up to about 1,100m. Diet comprises ants and spiders; a clutch size of four eggs is known, measuring 4.2–4.3 x 9.0–9.9mm, produced at intervals of about 100 days. Hatchlings measure 35–37mm. Endemic to Borneo, with records from Brunei, Sabah, Sarawak and Kalimantan.

Marquis Doria's Angle-headed Lizard *Gonocephalus doriae* 163mm

A brightly-coloured forest lizard from primary lowland forests. Body relatively robust; nuchal crest composed of low, overlapping and slightly crescentic scales; superciliary border distinctly raised; no spine-like scales on crest in adult males; dorsum green, changeable to reddish-brown with dark and light flecks; gular sac grey with dark stripes. Inhabits lowland rainforests, on low tree trunks and shrubs, and juveniles have been found asleep on leaves of saplings close to rivers. This rare lizard presumably feeds on small arthropods. Its breeding habits remain unknown, although like its relatives, it produces eggs. When threatened, it opens its mouth, without attempting to bite. Endemic to Borneo, and known from Sabah, Sarawak and Kalimantan.

Giant Angle-headed Lizard *Gonocephalus grandis* 160mm (males); 137mm (females)

A very large forest-dwelling lizard. Body robust; males with high nuchal and dorsal crests; the dorsal crest separated from the nuchal crest in males; females lack dorsal crest but show a nuchal sail; dorsals sub-equal, not with larger scales; ventrals smooth; dorsum greenish-brown, olive to nearly black, paler when unstressed and darker in stressed individuals; flanks blue, with yellow spots in males; females and juveniles brownish-green to black. Inhabits rainforests, up to an elevation of around 1,400m. Abundant in the vicinity of streams and small rivers, into which they are known to jump when threatened. Associated with tree trunks, although females and juveniles may also be found on rocky banks of streams, and sleeps at night on leaves of saplings or tips of twigs, especially those overhanging waterbodies. Diet comprises insects and other arthropods, including caterpillars, beetles, grasshoppers, ants, flies, cockroaches and spiders. Clutches of 1–6 eggs are laid several times a year, measuring 10–11 x 21–26mm, at intervals of 30–90 days. Incubation period is 75–90 days, and hatchlings measure 32–35mm. Known from Brunei, Sarawak, Sabah and Kalimantan, this species is widespread, from extreme southern Thailand, the Malay Peninsula, Sumatra, the Mentawai Archipelago and Borneo.

Blue-eyed Angle-headed Lizard *Gonocephalus liogaster*
140mm

Another large forest-dwelling lizard. Body robust; nuchal and dorsal crests continuous, comprising lanceolate scales; in females, nuchal crest long, dorsal crest low, ridge-like; supraciliary border rounded; dorsals intermixed with larger scales; a row of large scales below orbit of eye; males brown or green, with dark reticulate pattern on flanks; females with yellow cross-bars; eyes of males bright blue, the skin surrounding the orbit reddish-orange; in females, eyes are brown. Inhabits lowland rainforests, and also peat swamp forests. Diurnal activity on low vegetation such as tree trunks, generally in the vicinity of streams and small rivers. Diet comprises insects; clutches of 1–4 eggs are produced at a time, measuring 11 x 23mm, which hatch 97 days later. It has been reported from Brunei, Sarawak, Sabah and Kalimantan, the range of this lizard including Peninsular Malaysia, Sumatra and Borneo.

Mjöberg's Angle-headed Lizard *Gonocephalus mjobergi*
88mm

A poorly-known tree lizard from Gunung Murud, Sarawak. Body robust; supraciliary border not raised; tympanum equal to eye diameter; nostril within a single nasal; forehead scales feebly keeled; supralabials 8–9; infralabials eight; a single flat, large scale below tympanum; dewlap small, its edge feebly serrated and covered with small scales; nuchal crest present; dorsal crest a small ridge; dorsum pale green, changeable to brownish-grey, with narrow grey reticulate pattern, which, on lower flanks, encloses yellow spots; venter pale green. Known only from montane forests. Diet presumably comprises insects, though this and breeding habits unknown. Endemic to Borneo, where it occurs between 2,134–2,250m, the highest altitudinal record for a member of the genus.

Kinabalu Crested Dragon *Hypsicalotes kinabaluensis* 145mm

A large, dragon-like arboreal agamid from the middle (900–1,600m) elevations of Gunung Kinabalu. Body robust; limbs and tail long; sides of face with large scales about the size of orbit below tympanum; nuchal and dorsal crests present and separate from each other, continuing onto tail; midbody scale rows 51–54; large lanceolate scales forming a median row on gular pouch in males, which shows reduced, heterogenous scales; dewlap distinct in adult males, its scales small; distinct shoulder fold; dorsal scales heterogenous; and tail swollen basally, its posterior strongly compressed; forehead and dorsal surface of body green, trunk with chocolate-brown and black spots that form bands; gular pouch pale red with black and white stripes in anterior margin; venter brown with green spots; when threatened, the green dorsum is changeable to brown. Individuals are slow-moving, and the species may depend on crypsis for protection. Its diet and reproductive habits remain unknown. Its habitat includes highland dipterocarp to submontane forests. An endemic of Borneo.

Bornean Shrub Lizard *Phoxophrys borneensis* 155mm

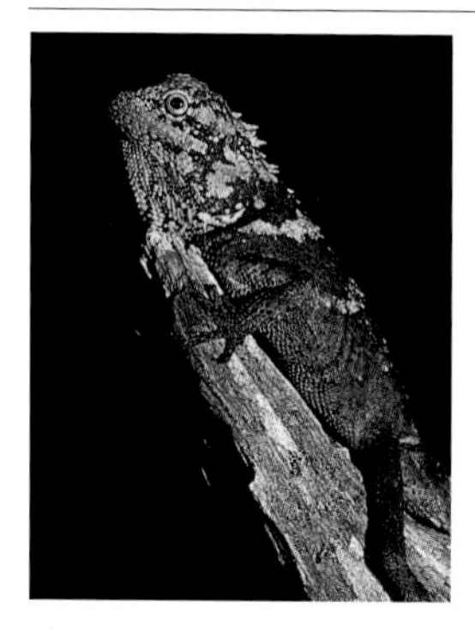

A small shrub-dwelling lizard. Body short, squat; spine above eyes absent; nasal in contact with supralabial; a continuous row of infraorbitals; gular scales sharply keeled; nuchal crest with four conical scales that are thick in males, compressed in females; an oblique axillary fold; an incomplete transverse gular fold; scales on sides of tail sharply keeled; four rows of keeled subcaudals near tail base; dorsum brown to greyish-brown, with yellowish-tan bands; two dark interorbital bars, the anterior narrower; upper lip cream; and inner lining of mouth deep blue. Inhabits montane forests between 1,300–1,800m. Diet presumably comprises insects; two eggs are produced at a time. Endemic to Borneo, with records from northern Sarawak, Sabah and central Kalimantan.

Large-headed Shrub Lizard *Phoxophrys cephalum* 84mm

Another lizard from high-elevation forests of Sabah's Kinabalu massif. Body short, squat; supraciliary spines absent; nuchal crest comprises 7–8 thick, conical scales; vertebral scale row comprises a few weakly-elevated, large, widely-separated scales posteriorly; nasal typically in contact with supralabials; two continuous rows of infraorbitals; gular scales obtusely keeled or smooth; five large scales on each side of expanded tail-base; enlarged spinous scales on outer edge of femur and forelimbs; ventrals keeled; two rows of large, keeled subcaudals; dorsum pale green, with dark green or greyish-green wavy bands, changeable to dark brown; large scales on nape yellow; two enlarged cream-coloured spines on sides of lower jaws; venter cream with dark green interscale markings joining to form stripes on greenish-cream throat; and inner lining of mouth deep blue. This slow-moving lizard inhabits submontane and montane forests, at elevations between 1,300–2,100m. When threatened, like other members of the genus, it opens its mouth, revealing the blue inner lining of the mouth, and may also become immobile for several minutes. Of its dietary habits, nothing is on record. Eggs measure 15.2–16.2 x 8.8–9.5mm, and four are laid at a time. Endemic to Borneo.

Black-lipped Shrub Lizard *Phoxophrys nigrilabris* 58mm

A short, squat lizard from shrubs in lowland forests. Body robust; spine above eyes absent; nuchal crest comprises 6–12 compressed scales; vertebral scale rows with a continuous series of large, raised scales posteriorly; nasal separated from supralabials; two continuous rows of infraorbitals; gular scales distinctly keeled; four rows of large scales near tail-base; dorsum of adult males brown with transverse blue bands; females and juveniles brown to olive; ventrally yellowish-cream, with dark brown vermiculations; and inner lining of mouth pale blue. The only lowland representative of the genus, and is associated with lowland dipterocarp forests, including disturbed areas. A diurnal, slow-moving, arboreal lizard, active on low tree trunks and shrubs. When threatened, it opens its mouth, revealing the blue-black lining of the mouth, and sometimes attempts to bite. Its diet includes insects and other arthropods. Reproductive habits are poorly known, and breeding may take place around the middle of the year. The range of the species includes Sarawak and western Kalimantan, and outside of Borneo, it is known from Pulau Sirhassen, in the Natuna Archipelago.

Spiny-headed Shrub Lizard *Phoxophrys spiniceps* 60.3mm

A montane lizard from shrubs, known only from Gunung Murud and Gunung Mulu in Sarawak. Body short, squat; enlarged spine above eyes; nasal in contact with second supralabial; infraorbitals in a single continuous row; gular scales keeled; nuchal crest comprises three scales separated by 2–6 small, keeled scales; an oblique fold in front of shoulder; vertebral scale row with widely separated large scales posteriorly; two rows of enlarged, keeled subcaudals; dorsum greenish-grey with brown patches, changeable to brown, with thin, pale transverse lines meeting at vertebral region; venter spotted with grey; dewlap bright yellow; and inner lining of mouth, including tongue deep blue. Inhabits high altitudes (altitudes of 1,200–1,800m) of north-central Sarawak, and adjacent areas of Sabah, in northern Borneo. When threatened, it opens its mouth, revealing the deep blue mouth lining. Diet presumably comprises arthropods; two eggs, measuring 12 x 7mm, are produced at a time. Endemic to Borneo.

ANGUIDAE (GLASS SNAKES)

Glass snakes are small to large-growing, limbless lizards, heavily armoured with largely non-overlapping scales that are underlain by rectangular osteoderms and typically with a longitudinal ventrolateral fold that separates the dorsal and ventral armour on each side. The tail is autotomized when threatened. Carnivorous in dietary habits, they are predominantly terrestrial or semi-fossorial. The single Bornean species is known from moist lowland as well as high altitude pine-oak forests.

Bornean Glass Snake *Ophisaurus buettikoferi* 125mm

A limbless lizard from middle elevations and lowlands of Borneo. Body slender; limbs externally absent; frontal and interparietal form a wide suture; supraoculars five; tympanum distinct; dorsals in 16–18 longitudinal rows and 98–105 transverse row; the central 12 rows of dorsals keeled to form unbroken straight lines; ventrals smooth, in 10 longitudinal rows; caudals keeled; ear-opening distinct; teeth conical; dorsally brown, with a dark lateral band, edged with light above, continuing to tail; a small blue interparietal spot; front portion of back with irregular transverse series of blue spots, edged anteriorly with black; five oblique dark lines across labials; and labials and venter pale yellow. A terrestrial and probably semi-fossorial, diurnal lizard, known from isolated localities at elevations of about 300 and 1,600m. Little is known of its diet and reproductive habits; the remains of a cockroach and the fragment of a rat's leg were found within one, the latter foodstuff presumably obtained through scavenging. Records of this species are from Sarawak's Batang Lemanak and Lantjak-Entimau Wildlife Sanctuary; Sabah's Gunung Kinabalu Park and Long Pasia, Sipitang District, and Kalimantan's Bukit Liang Kubung, and Taman Nasional Kayan Mentarang. A Bornean endemic.

EUBLEPHARIDAE (EYELID GECKOS)

Formerly, eublepharid geckos were placed with the typical geckos in the same family, but they differ in several fundamental features, such as showing fleshy eyelids and eggs with leathery shells. A single species occurs on Borneo, the distribution of this family including both the New and the Old Worlds. Most species (except the Bornean and the east Asian ones, which are forest dwellers) inhabit scrub forests and deserts. All feed on invertebrates. One species in this family, the Indian Leopard Gecko, *Eublepharis macularius*, shows temperature-dependent sex determination.

Cat Gecko *Aeluroscalabotes felinus* 122mm

A brightly-coloured forest-dwelling lizard with a prehensile tail-tip. Body slender; eyelids fleshy; tail rounded and capable of being curled laterally; axillary pockets absent; large retractable claw on each digit between one dorsal and two lateral scutes; transverse enlarged lamellae restricted to base of digits; dorsum reddish-brown, more brightly-coloured in juveniles, with white spots and vertebral stripe on body and tail; sometimes, tail-tip is white. Inhabits lowland rainforests and peat swamp forests, up to about 1,000m. Slow-moving and arboreal, it is active on low vegetation of saplings and dead logs at night. Its diet comprises arthropods, such as crickets and cockroaches; between one to two elongate eggs with parchment shells, measuring 9.5–13 x 17.0–21.2mm, are produced. Incubation period is 35–64 days, hatchlings measuring 78–81mm. Known from Sarawak, Sabah and Kalimantan, this unusual lizard ranges from Peninsular Thailand, the Malay Peninsula, to Sumatra and Borneo.

GEKKONIDAE (TRUE GECKOS)

Geckos are familiar to all city dwellers – this family includes species commonly found in human dwellings. House geckos actually include several species, and many are commensals of humans. However, most species of geckos are found in undisturbed habitats, from forests to scrubland and even on desert dunes. All species are primarily insectivorous, tending to sit in wait for insects of appropriate size to come within striking distance. Their tails are detachable, a new one replacing the one that is lost.

Kendall's Day Gecko *Cnemaspis kendallii* 80mm

A forest-dwelling, day-active gecko. Body slender; canthal ridge well-developed, extending backwards over the orbit; postnasals six; postmentals reduced; pectoral and abdominal scales distinctly elongated, imbricate and unicarinate; tail with a median row of pointed semi-erect scales below; supralabials 10–12; infralabials 8–11; interorbital scale rows nine; midventrals 40; dorsum with larger and small scattered scales; median subcaudals tricarinate; males lacking preanal or femoral pores or preanal groove; two postcloacal spurs; dorsum pale brown, with dark brown oblong spots forming seven interrupted bands. Inhabits lowland forests, peat swamps and midhills up to an elevation of 1,310m. When alarmed, they curl their tail over their backs, perhaps a defensive mimicry of scorpions. Tail curling also has a role in social interactions, used to intimidate rivals, along with head-bobbing. Its diet includes ants, earthworms, beetles and millipedes. It produces two eggs at a time. Known from the Malay Peninsula, including Pulau Tioman, the Riau and Natuna Archipelagos and north-western Borneo (Sarawak).

Gading Day Gecko *Cnemaspis nigridia* 69.8mm

A rock-dwelling gecko, from isolated mountains of western Sarawak. Body robust; canthal ridge developed; five postnasals; postmentals large; pectoral and abdominal scales imbricate and tricarinate; supralabials 11; infralabials 12; midventrals 68; median subcaudals smooth; dorsum with small granular scales and scattered large keeled tubercles; males typically without preanal or femoral pores, or preanal groove; one or two postcloacal spurs; tail without a median row of pointed scales below; dorsal surface brownish-olive, with black blotches, especially on scapular region; two pairs of dark brown elongated spots on nape and axilla; a single elongated spot on vertebral region; some scales on middorsum green in life; and venter unpatterned grey. Inhabits granite and limestone hills of western Sarawak, between low to middle elevations (500–ca.1,100m). Diet comprises spiders and presumably other arthropods. Two eggs are produced at a time, measuring 9.8–11.2 x 8.4–10.2mm, laid communally on rocky substrates such as caves and rock crevices. Endemic to north-western Borneo (Gunung Gading, Gunung Pueh and the limestone hills of the Bau region) and Natuna Island.

Frilly Forest Gecko *Hemidactylus craspedotus* 62mm

A frilled gecko from lowland rainforests. Body slender; body and tail depressed; dorsum with scattered tubercles; skin frills on sides of body, tail, sides of throat and along lateral edges of limbs; digits nearly fully-webbed; dorsal surface greyish-brown, with two rows of dark, rectangular spots; a dark streak along side of head; tail with dark bands on the upper surface, its lower surface reddish-orange basally, greyish-yellow distally; and venter bright yellow, speckled with dark brown. Inhabits trees in rainforests and is insectivorous. Generally nocturnal or crepuscular, it is active on tree trunks, individuals sometimes seen abroad during the day. The lateral dermal frills of the body are well-developed, and may be both for camouflage and for movement: this species is known to both parachute and glide for distances up to 3m between trees. Of its reproductive habits, nothing is known. This poorly-known gecko has been recorded from Sarawak and Sabah, and extralimitally, from Peninsular Thailand, the Malay Peninsula and Borneo, and probably also from Java.

Frilly House Gecko *Hemidactylus platyurus* 69mm

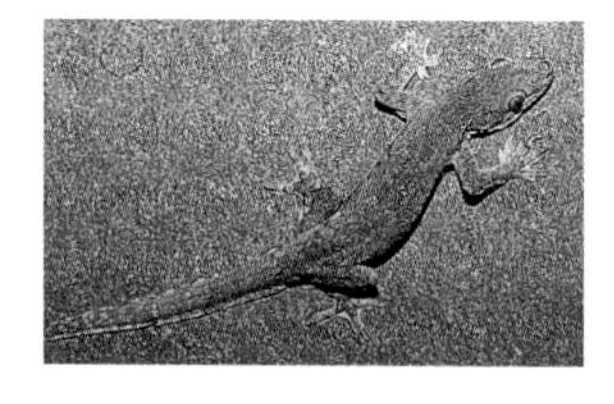

A familiar house gecko in Borneo. Body slender; fingers and toes about half-webbed; a fringe of skin on sides of body and back of hindlimbs; tail flattened, with a serrated margin; body depressed, smooth, with tiny granules; lamellae under toe IV 7–9; males with 34–36 femoral pores; dorsum light grey, sometimes with darker markings; a dark grey streak between eye and shoulder; and venter unpatterned yellow. A human commensal, abundant in towns and cities, but also known from lowland forests and trees along sea-coasts. By day, they hide behind bookshelves and in cracks in the woodwork, emerging at dusk to wait in ambush for arthropods, usually close to electric light-bulbs and other brightly-lit parts of the wall. Parachuting and gliding behaviour known in the species. Its territorial call is a chuckling sound, with 4–5 notes uttered in quick succession. Diet comprises spiders and ants. Two eggs, measuring 10.0–10.8 x 8.5–8.9mm, are produced at a time, several clutches being laid every year. Hatchlings are 20.5–25mm. Known from all parts of Borneo. A widely distributed species, its range extends from eastern India, Nepal, Andaman and Nicobar Islands, Sri Lanka, southern China, to all of South-east Asia to Sulawesi and the Philippines; introduced into Papua New Guinea.

Kinabalu Bent-toed Gecko *Cyrtodactylus baluensis* 86mm

A tree gecko from northern Borneo. Body slender; dorsals small, with larger tubercles in 21–24 rows; supralabials 10–12; infralabials 9–10; midventrals 40–45; preanal groove absent; preanal pores 9–10, forming a narrow angular series within a distinct depression and separated by femoral pores; femoral pores 6–9; a sharp boundary of scale size between the large ventral scales and the posterior scales that are granular; lamellae under toe IV 21–23; dorsum brown to yellowish-brown with irregular dark spots that may form dark cross-bars; head with dark brown lateral band from snout-tip to nape; limbs and tail dark-banded. Inhabits dipterocarp rainforests to montane oak forests, between 150–2,500m. Nocturnal, forages on leaves of saplings, and more rarely, on tree trunks, buttresses and forest clearings, while hiding under loose bark and fallen trees during the day. Diet comprises insects and other arthropods; two eggs are produced at a time, measuring 12 x 15mm, which are deposited in the soil at the base of trees; hatchlings measure 31–32mm. Endemic to northern Borneo, especially the highlands of Sabah, as well as adjacent Sarawak, Brunei and possibly eastern Kalimantan.

Niah Cave Gecko *Cyrtodactylus cavernicolus* 80.8mm

A forest gecko restricted to the limestone regions of Niah and Mulu, in northern Sarawak. Body slender; preanal grooves containing two pairs of pores; dorsal surface covered with small, granular scales interspersed with 20–22 rows of trihedral or conical tubercles; femoral pores and large femoral scales absent; lamellae under toe IV 22–26; dorsum brown, with dark-edged brown cross-bars, changeable to brown-black; a dark stripe from corner of eyes to nape; venter unpatterned cream; and tail dark-banded. Inhabits lowland forests and caves in northern Sarawak. Within cave systems, it is found both on walls as well as on wooden man-made structures, such as walkways and ladders placed by collectors of swiftlet nests. Juveniles have also been found under fallen tree trunks on the forest floor. Its diet comprises flattened cave cockroaches and moths that dwell in guano. Reproductive habits remain unknown. Endemic to north-western Borneo.

Peters' Bent-toed Gecko *Cyrtodactylus consobrinus* 125mm

A large, forest gecko associated with mature trees in lowland dipterocarp forests. Body robust; dorsum with scattered tuberculate scales in 18–20 irregular rows; supralabials 10–16; infralabials 9–13; midventrals 58–70; femoral pores large, numbering up to six; males and females with 9–14 preanal scales forming a narrow angular series, pores present only in males; preanal groove absent; forehead with pale narrow network of reticulations; dorsum dark chocolate-brown with 4–8 white or yellow transverse bands; juveniles have similar pattern, but the ground colour is bright yellow. Inhabits lowland dipterocarp forests up to 1,100m, and also enters limestone caves; diet comprises insects. Two eggs, measuring 14.0–17.6mm, are produced several times a year. Hatchlings measuring 31mm. Known from Brunei, Sarawak, Sabah and Kalimantan. This familiar forest gecko is restricted to the Malay Peninsula, Sumatra, Sinkep and Borneo.

Inger's Bent-toed Gecko *Cyrtodactylus ingeri* 80.2mm

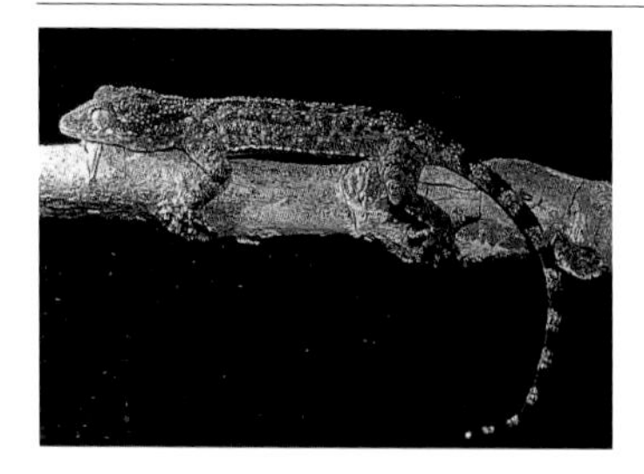

A forest gecko from northern and north-western Borneo. Body slender; dorsum with large, tuberculate scales in 17 irregular rows; rounded imbricate ventrals; supralabials 10–12; infralabials 8–10; midventrals 40–43; lamellae under toe IV 23–28; males with 7–9 preanal pores forming a narrow angular series; femoral pores and preanal groove absent; dorsum grey or yellowish-brown, with 5–6 irregular dark brown diamond-shaped paired paravertebral blotches that are sometimes fused; on flanks, a short, interrupted, dark brown stripe; nape typically with a dark Y- or V-shaped mark; a pale brown postocular stripe from posterior edge of eye to insertion of forearm; iris yellow; supralabials and infralabials yellow-cream; tongue pale pink, with a grey-pink tip; upper surface of digits and limbs with dark blotches, that of tail with dark bands; throat yellow-cream; and rest of venter cream. Inhabits riparian forests, between 500–800m, its diet presumably comprises arthropods. Two eggs, measuring 12 x 9mm, are produced at a time. Known from Sabah and Brunei Darussalam; endemic to Borneo.

Malayan Bent-toed Gecko *Cyrtodactylus malayanus* 117mm

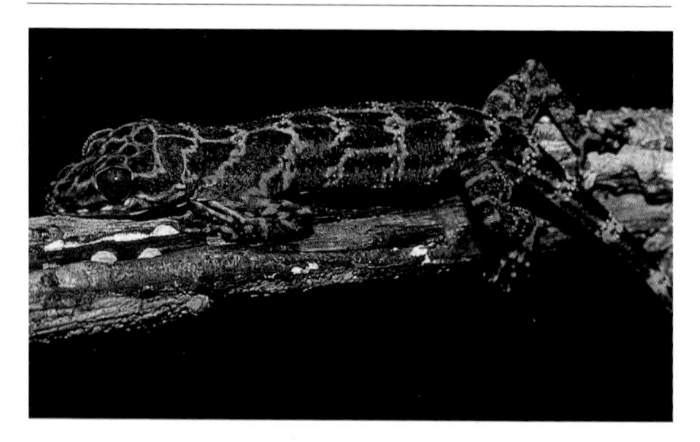

A rare forest-dwelling gecko from the interiors of Borneo. Body robust; preanal groove absent; preanal pores indistinct in males; subcaudals large; forehead with a pale network of reticulations; narrow light cross-bars on dorsum of body; a series of isolated dark spots along vertebral region; venter grey. Arboreal and nocturnal, this poorly-known species is found on large trees in lowland dipterocarp forests, and may descend to 1.5 m above ground. Its diet and reproductive habits remain unstudied. This understudied gecko has been recorded from Sarawak, Brunei and Kalimantan, and is endemic to Borneo.

Matsui's Bent-toed Gecko *Cyrtodactylus matsuii* 105mm

A large gecko from the mountains of Sabah. Body stout; supralabials 10–12; infralabials 10–11; dorsals with large, tuberculate scales arranged in 18 irregular rows; midventrals 48–51; males with 7–8 preanal pores forming a wide angular series; preanal groove absent; lamellae under toe IV 22; subdigital lamellae widened; dorsum yellowish-brown or pale brown, with irregular dark cross-bars; forehead with small dark spots; dark band on interorbital region joining posterior edge of eyes; upper surface of limbs and tail dark-banded; and venter pale grey or brown, unpatterned. Inhabits forests at elevations between 900–1,600m, its diet comprises insects and other arthropods. Nothing is on record of its reproductive habits. This gecko is endemic to northern Borneo.

Grooved Bent-toed Gecko *Cyrtodactylus pubisulcus* 77mm

A common lowland gecko from western Borneo. Body slender; a ventro-lateral dermal fold present; supra-labials 10–11; mid-ventrals 43–55; preanal groove present; preanal pores 3–5 pairs; dorsal tubercles not in regular longitudinal rows; subcaudals not transversely arranged; dorsum grey, dark markings on dorsal surface arranged in the form of cross-bars or blotches, sometimes arranged in a longitudinal series. Inhabits lowland rainforests and peat swamps; its diet comprises insects such as cockroaches; two eggs, measuring 10.0–13.0mm, are produced at a time. Restricted to the western and north-western part of Borneo, within Sarawak and Brunei Darussalam, this species is an endemic of Borneo.

Striped Bent-toed Gecko *Cyrtodactylus quadrivirgatus* 71mm

A lowland gecko from western Borneo, within Sarawak State. Body slender; supralabials 10; infralabials 10; midventrals 40; dorsal tubercles arranged in regular longitudinal rows; males with four preanal pores; preanal groove absent; median series of widened subcaudals absent; dorsum grey or dark brown, with four black longitudinal lines, separated by lighter areas; no continuous black band joining the eyes. Inhabiting primary and secondary forests, its diet comprises arthropods. Two eggs are produced at a time and hatchlings measure 25–26mm. This widespread species is known from southern Thailand, the Malay Peninsula, northern Sumatra, the Mentawai Archipelago and north-western Borneo.

Yoshi's Bent-toed Gecko *Cyrtodactylus yoshii* 96mm

A large, lowland gecko from Sabah. Body robust, supralabials 10–14; midventrals 50–58; males without femoral pores; preanal pores 8–12, forming a narrow angular series; preanal groove absent; lamellae under toe IV 25–30; subdigital lamellae not widened; dorsum grey, with five dark V-shaped cross-bars between nape and inguinal region; a dark brown V-shaped stripe extends from posterior corner of orbit of eye, through the top of the ear opening, meeting on the nape; lips white-spotted; dorsal surfaces of limbs with indistinct dark bands. Inhabits lowland forests and found on tree trunks and walls of human-made structures within forests. The diet of this rare species presumably comprises large insects. Reproductive habits unknown. It is endemic to northern Borneo.

Four-clawed House Gecko *Gehyra mutilata* 64mm

A common house gecko, with a delicate skin. Body slender; head relatively large and oval; midventrals 35–44; tail distinctly flattened dorsoventrally, widening at base, with sharp, somewhat denticulate edges; males with 25–41 preanofemoral pores; lamellae under toe IV 25; postanal tubercle absent; dorsum pale grey, usually with a paler vertebral area, with dark and light spots. Inhabits both human habitations and primary forests, its call is a series of 6–8 monosyllabic 'tock' sounds that increase in intensity. When captured, it does not attempt to bite, but defacates as an antipredator response. Its diet comprises insects and isopods and 1–2 eggs, measuring 7.1–8.5 x 10.5–11.2mm, are produced at a time. Incubation period is 54–60 days and hatchlings measure 17–23mm. Known from all parts of Borneo, the global distribution of this species is wide but patchy: mainland South-east Asia, east to New Guinea and the Philippines, and also India and Sri Lanka; this gecko has been introduced into Mauritius, Seychelles, Madagascar, Mexico, Cuba and Hawai'i.

Tokay Gecko *Gekko gecko* 176mm

A noisy tree gecko from small islands to the north of Borneo, and from other isolated localities on this island. Body robust; head relatively large; body with granular scales; supralabials and infralabials with weak keels; males with 10–24 preanal pores; femoral pores present; dorsum slaty-grey to bluish-grey, with red or orange spots. Mostly restricted to offshore islands, such as those north of Sabah. It inhabits coastal forests and is active at night on tree trunks. The loud call of this gecko can be syllabilized as 'Tock-ay', uttered 4–9 times in slow succession, and heard both by day and at night. Diet includes moths, grasshoppers, beetles, spiders, other geckos, small mice and snakes; and 1–2 eggs, measuring 19–21 x 15–17mm, are laid in tree holes. Hatchlings measure 39.8–42.3mm. Known from Pulau Bohey Dulang, Pulau Balambangan, Pulau Banggi, all in Sabah, besides isolated locations in southern, central and eastern Kalimantan. The distribution of this gecko is from eastern India, Nepal, Bangladesh, east to southern China and South-east Asia, to the Philippines; introduced into Florida and Hawai'i, Martinique in the West Indies, and Madagascar.

Warty House Gecko *Gekko monarchus* 102mm

A large, rough, house gecko. Body robust and tuberculate; dorsals with large, tuberculate scales arranged in 16–17 longitudinal rows; scales on throat granular; midventrals 30–38; supralabials 10–11; infralabials 9–12; digits widened, basally webbed; weak webbing between toes IV and V; preanofemoral pores 23–42; median row of subcaudals widened; dorsum greyish-brown, with dark brown blotches arranged in 7–9 pairs; inhabits both buildings and forest edges up to 1,500m. Vocalisations comprise 51 individual, low, 'tock-tock' calls. Diet comprises insects and other invertebrates, and two eggs are produced at a time, measuring 9.3–13.6 x 9.5–11.4mm, and attached to rock crevices. Communal nesting in the species known; over 50 eggs have been found. Incubation period is 120 days and hatchlings measure 25–30mm. The distribution of this lizard extends from southern Thailand, the Malay Peninsula, Sumatra, the Mentawai Archipelago, Pulau Simeulue, Borneo (including all parts of this island), Java, Maluku and the Philippines.

Smith's Giant Gecko *Gekko smithii* 180mm

A large forest gecko, whose barking call is unmistakable. Body robust; head large; body thick-set, with scattered tubercles on dorsal surface; males with 11–16 preanal pores in a short angular series; dorsal surface greyish-brown or pale greyish-yellow, with a transverse series of white spots, composed of white-tipped tubercles and their surrounding areas; cream-coloured bands on sagittal and nuchal regions; iris pale green, pupil black, vertical; tongue pale pink, apically grey; tail with cream bands. It inhabits forested-habitats in the lowlands as well as the midhills, its call is reminiscent of a dog's bark, comprising one to three short barks, typically followed by a whirring sound. Diet comprises insects, such as grasshoppers and two eggs, measuring 19 x 20mm, are laid at a time. Reported from Brunei, Sarawak, Sabah and Kalimantan. The distribution of this lizard includes the Nicobar Islands, southern Thailand, the Malay Peninsula, Sumatra, Borneo, Pulau Nias and Java.

Brooke's House Gecko *Hemidactylus brookii* 63mm

A gecko from disturbed habitats, and only a single Bornean population is known. Body robust, flattened; with rows of tubercles; tail with spiny tubercles; tail plump with spine-like tubercles on dorsal surface; males with 7–12 preanofemoral pores; dorsal surface dark brown to light grey; with dark spots usually arranged in groups; two dark lines along nostrils and eyes; and venter cream. On the Asian mainland, it inhabits parks, gardens, houses, as well as forests. Its loud 'chuck-chuck-chuck' call is commonly heard after dark, and its diet comprises small insects; two eggs are produced at a time, 7 x 9mm, and more than a single clutch may be laid, eggs hatching in about 43 days. Widely distributed in South-east Asia, with introduced populations in the Indian subcontiennt. In Borneo, the only extant population is in Loagan Bunut, in northern Sarawak, although it was described on the basis of specimens taken from this island.

Asian House Gecko *Hemidactylus frenatus* 67mm

A common house gecko from towns and cities in Borneo. Body slender, depressed; fingers and toes unwebbed; dorsal scales smooth; sides of tail rounded, relatively long, with large tubercles; no flaps of skin along sides of body and at back of hindlimbs; supralabials 10–12; infralabials 7–10; preanofemoral pores in males 28–36; dorsum yellowish-brown to almost black, with darker markings; a light-edged brown streak along sides of head. Inhabits man-made structures as well as forested areas, from sea level to nearly 1,600m. Its call is a series of 4–5 loud, staccato notes. Diet includes insects and spiders and two eggs are produced at a time, measuring 8.2–10.0 x 7.2–8.4mm, that hatch in 46–62 days to produce hatchlings of 46–60mm. Widespread from India, Sri Lanka, southern China, to South-east Asia and introduced into Central and South America, Madagascar, eastern and southern Africa, Mauritius, New Guinea, Polynesia and Australia.

Worm Gecko *Hemiphyllodactylus typus* 47mm

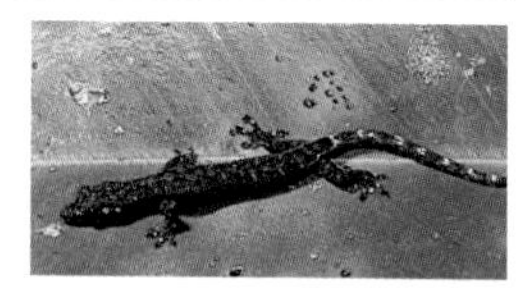

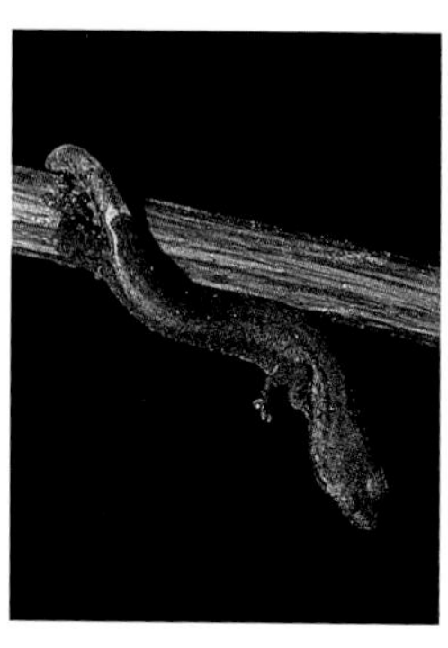

A worm-like, tree-dwelling gecko. Body slender and depressed; limbs reduced; granular dorsal scales, but lacking tubercles; ventral scales smooth, rounded and imbricate; digits free; scansors divided, numbering 3–6; supralabials 8–12; infralabials 8–12; tail slender, prehensile, dorsum brown; a dark brown stripe from nostril to shoulder; a light V-shaped mark at base of tail. Inhabits lowland forests and mangroves, up to an altitude of nearly 1,000m; diet comprises small insects. An all-female species, producing two eggs, measuring 8 x 6mm, without mating. Hatchlings 33– 35mm in length. Recorded from Brunei, Sarawak, Sabah and Kalimantan, this species is widespread in tropical Asia and the Indo-Pacific, from Mauritius, Andaman and Nicobar Islands, Sri Lanka, Myanmar, China, east through South-east Asia to New Guinea, Solomon Islands, New Caledonia, Polynesia, Hawai'i and the Mascarene Islands.

Common Mourning Gecko *Lepidodactylus lugubris* 49mm

Another all-female species of tree lizard. Body slender and elongated, with a wide tail; tubercles on dorsal surface absent; preano-femoral scales 25–31; terminal scansors divided, moderately expanded; tail as long as or longer than combined length of head and body, wide at base, transversely flattened; dorsum cinnamon-brown, pale brown or greyish-brown; pale transverse sinous pattern on dorsum, especially at pelvic region; a small black blotch on each side of pelvic region. Inhabits lowland, including coastal forests, in particular mangroves. Its diet includes insects, although nectar and plant juice are also lapped up. 1–2 eggs are produced without mating, eggs measuring 7.0-8.7 x 9.5-10mm. Hatchlings measure 17.2–17.8mm and emerge after 60–117 days of incubation. Bornean records are from coastal areas of Sarawak, Sabah and Kalimantan. Members of this species complex are known from the Maldives, Andaman and Nicobar Islands, Sri Lanka, southern China, east through South-east Asia to New Guinea, and the South Pacific; introduced into Panama, Ecuador, Galapagos Islands and Central America.

Kinabalu Mourning Gecko *Lepidodactylus ranauensis* 47.7mm

A house gecko from the hills of northern Borneo. Body slender, depressed, with a wide tail; dorsals small, lacking large tubercles; supralabials nine; infralabials 9–10; midbody scale rows 108; digits long, relatively narrow; ventral surface with scansors on distal four-fifths; terminal lamellae entire; lamellae under toe IV 14–15; males with a continuous series of 35–37 preanofemoral pores; femoral pores extending almost to distal edge of thighs; cloacal spur single; tail subcylindrical, lacking lateral ornamentation; dorsum greyish-brown; forehead greyish-brown or with a slightly reddish-brown area; a pair of dark triangular markings on dorsolateral part of tail base; and venter greyish-tan. Only known from walls of buildings, its diet presumably comprises insects; two eggs, measuring 4.1 x 3.7 and 4.5 x 3.6mm, are produced at a time. This species is endemic to Sabah, in northern Borneo, and known only from the middle elevations and foothills of Gunung Kinabalu.

Brown's Camouflage Gecko *Luperosaurus browni* 66.5mm

A poorly-known tree-dwelling gecko. Body slender; skin folds present on limbs; ventrals flat, subimbricate; lamellae entire, numbering 16–19 under toe IV; preanofemoral pores 28–32; digits strongly dilated and half-webbed; first digit unclawed; tail depressed with lateral spines; dorsum light grey, with minute black spots on head, body and limbs; a dark stripe in supralabial region; five dark broken chevrons on middorsum of body; tail dark-banded; and venter white with several dark spots on tail. Inhabits lowland rainforests and diet presumably comprises small insects. Two eggs, measuring 8.1–9.6 x 8.8–8.9mm, produce hatchlings 28.3–29.3mm. Known from isolated localities in the Malay Peninsula and northern and central Borneo (Sarawak and Kalimantan).

Yasuma's Camouflage Gecko *Luperosaurus yasumai* 38.9mm

A rare gecko, known only from Bukit Soeharto Experimental Forest, in the vicinity of Samarinda, East Kalimantan. Body slender; head depressed; snout strongly tapered; supralabials 9–10; infralabials 10–11; dorsal tubercles conical or spinose; ventrals flat, subimbricate; lamellae entire; tail strongly depressed; dorsal surface of head and tail yellowish-brown, of body brownish-tan; numerous pale, cloudy markings on head, body and tail; two distinct, rounded, ivory spots on middorsum; venter light grey with several dark dots in the gular region; and eight indistinct dark broad bands on tail. The only specimen of this species was found on a path through regenerating dipterocarp forest, where it was lying motionless. Nothing is known of its biology, except that eggs are produced in December.

Horsfield's Gliding Gecko *Ptychozoon horsfieldii* 80mm

A parachuting gecko from the lowlands of Borneo. Body robust; dorsal tubercles absent; femoral pores 8–11; preanal pores 10–11; femoral and preanal pores in separated series; 21–22 denticulate tail lobes; tail lobe size reduction to tail-tip gradual; dorsum grey to medium brown, peppered with black mottlings, with a dark brown wavy pattern, forehead and upper surfaces of limbs and digits grey with black mottlings; a broad dark band from posterior corner of eyes to beyond tympanum; two large oval blotches that reach insertion of forelimbs; a dark butterfly-shaped mark on axilla; trunk with three other wavy bands; dorsal surface of patagium yellowish-brown, with five pale brown bands; chin yellow with a few scattered brown spots. Inhabits lowland rainforests as well as man-made structures. Its diet presumably comprises small insects. Two eggs, 13.7 x 11.9mm, are produced and hatchlings measure 34mm. Known from a few isolated records in Borneo, including Brunei, Sarawak, Sabah and Kalimantan, this species is widely distributed from Myanmar, Thailand, the Malay Peninsula, to Sumatra and Borneo.

Kuhl's Gliding Gecko *Ptychozoon kuhli* 107.8mm

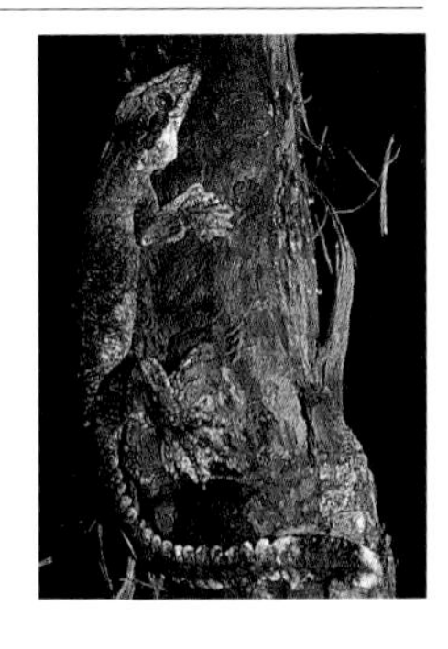

Another parachuting gecko from the lowlands. Body robust; scattered granules on dorsal surface of body that are strongly convex, raised or spinose; tail lappets set at right angles to tail; widely expanded non-denticulate terminal tail-flap; large skin expansions on the sides of the body; femoral pores absent; preanal pores 14–32, oriented in a curved line; dorsal surface grey or reddish-brown, with 4–5 wave wavy transverse bands of dark brown on trunk; a dark brown line from eye to first dorsal band; and venter unpatterned yellow. Inhabits large trees in lowland forests, up to at least 35m above ground, and occasionally, enters walls of houses. Diet includes arthropods, including grasshoppers and two eggs, measuring 10–15mm, are glued to tree trunks and branches. Incubation period is 73–100 days, although a five-month incubation period is also known. Hatchlings measure 34mm. Recorded from Brunei, Sarawak, Sabah and Kalimantan. This familiar gecko is known from southern Thailand, the Malay Peninsula, Sumatra, the Mentawai Archipelago, Java and Borneo.

Kinabalu Wall Gecko *Ptychozoon rhacophorus* 75mm

A montane arboreal gecko, restricted to the Kinabalu Massif in Sabah. Body relatively robust; dorsal surface with spinose or thorny tubercles that are widely scattered; skin on sides of body jagged and irregularly-lobed; ventrals granular; supralabials nine; infralabials 10; supranasals widely separated; head lacks lateral skin fringes; sharply tapered tail which is short and without distinct lobes; terminal expansion of tail absent; reduced digital webbing; preanal pores 17; femoral pores absent; postanal tubercles 2–3; dorsum brownish-green, unpatterned or with dark mottlings and indistinct wavy bands; and venter light brown, speckled with dark brown. Inhabits montane regions, where it is observed on walls of buildings and on trunks of large trees, at altitudes between 600–1,600m. Nocturnal and insectivorous, being known to eat moths. Nothing is known of its reproductive biology.

LACERTIDAE (LACERTAS)

Lacertas are primarily lizards of colder, open areas of Europe and central Asia. A single species occurs on Borneo. They are rough-scaled, with enlarged forehead scales, well-developed limbs and show femoral pores. These are fast-moving and diurnal predators of insects and other small invertebrates.

Long-tailed Grass Lizard *Takydromus sexlineatus* 61mm

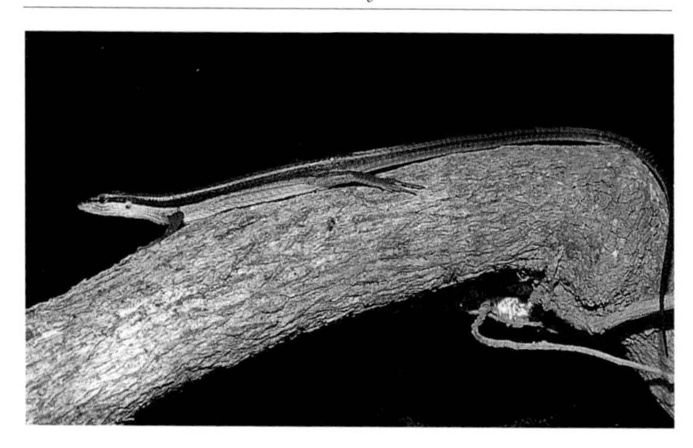

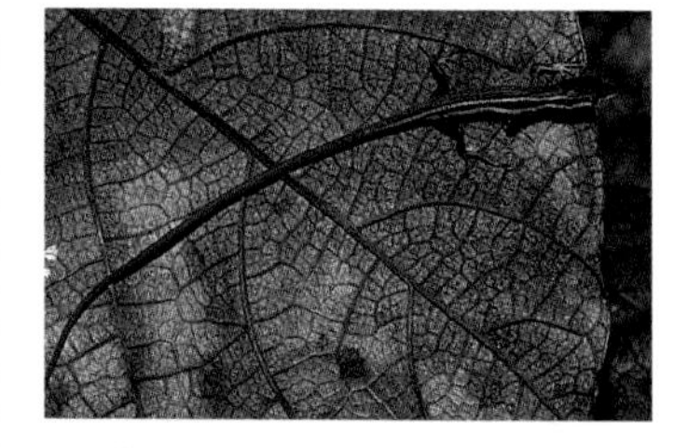

A long-tailed lizard from grasslands of western Borneo. Body long and slender; head long; dorsal surface with large, smooth, plate-like scales; tail between 3–5 times as long as body; sides of body with a single row of large scales; transverse scale rows and plates 40; 1–2 femoral pores; dorsal surface striped, including a coffee-brown vertebral stripe from forehead, a yellow stripe from orbit to flanks of body; a paravertebral stripe extends beyond tail-base; dorsolateral stripe dark brown, unpatterned; flanks greenish-yellow in the anterior first third of length; venter with a pale brown sheen; males brighter than females in colouration; and juveniles resembling adult females. Inhabits grasslands and marshes, where it feeds on insects and millipedes. Clutches of 2–3 eggs, measuring 10–11 x 6–7mm, are produced; hatchlings are 23mm. Within Borneo, this species is restricted to Sarawak and Kalimantan, its distribution ranging from north-eastern India, Myanmar, Thailand, Vietnam, southern and eastern China, to Borneo, Sumatra and Java.

LANTHANOTIDAE (BORNEAN EARLESS MONITOR)

A family of enigmatic lizards, containing a single species, that is endemic to Borneo. It has short limbs; a somewhat prehensile tail; nostrils are moved backwards and upwards as an adaptation to its semiaquatic lifestyle. Eyes reduced with moveable lids, lower lid transparent; ear-opening absent and palatine teeth present. Endemic to Borneo.

Bornean Earless Monitor *Lanthanotus borneensis* 200mm

A small, slender, elongated lizard, its closest relatives are the monitor lizards. Body slender, elongate and cylindrical, with short limbs; head blunt; forehead flat, covered with small granular, nodule-like scales; nostrils situated on upper surface of snout; eyes reduced, with moveable lids; lower eyelid with transparent window; tongue forked; males with blunt, rectangular jaws; females with relatively pointed jaws; heterogenous scalation with underlying osteoderms, including six parallel rows of large tuberculate scales on dorsal surface from the head to the back of the body; two central rows of large scales on tail; dorsum unpatterned brownish-orange, or with a dark vertebral stripe. Inhabits lowlands near streams, and also agricultural lands. Apparently nocturnal, daylight hours being spent in retreats such as burrows in the soil up to about 30cm, reportedly along riverbanks or under rocks and fallen logs. At night, it forages on land and in water. Locomotion, especially underwater is via undulatory movements. Diet comprises earthworms and crustaceans. Between 2–5 oval eggs, measuring 30mm are produced at a time. Restricted to Sarawak and Kalimantan, in western Borneo.

SCINCIDAE (SKINKS)

Skinks are shiny-scaled, diurnal lizards, found scurrying on the forest floor wherever there are patches of sunlight filtering in. This is one of the largest families of lizards, and found on all continents. They actively search for prey on the surface of soil (a few species are arboreal), which comprises insects and other small invertebrates. Those that are fossorial are poorly known. Most skinks have smooth scales, possibly adapted for burrowing in soil, and all have detachable tails, that regenerate eventually.

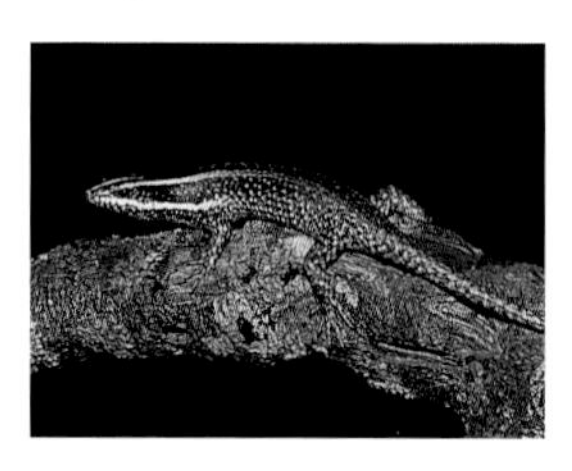

Striped Bornean Tree Skink *Apterygodon vittatum* 96mm

A familiar tree skink in the lowlands. Body robust; dorsals keeled; prefrontals separated from each other; frontal larger than frontoparietal and interparietal; nuchals generally absent, and when present, only a single pair; supraoculars five; supraciliaries 8–9; supralabials 7–8; tympanum present; midbody scale rows 30; scales under toe IV 16–22; two large heel scales in males; tail rounded in cross-section, tapering to a fine point; head and anterior of body black; rest of dorsum brownish-grey; with dark and light spots; a light cream or yellow stripe from snout-tip to back of head; a pale stripe from above eyes to along body; and venter green. Inhabits lowland rainforests, as well as parks and gardens, ascending large trees up to about 37m. Its diet is primarily ants, and also other small insects; and 2–4 thick-shelled eggs are produced at a time. The genus, with a single species, is endemic to Borneo, where it is widespread, being recorded from Brunei, Sarawak, Sabah and Kalimantan.

Grey Tree Skink *Dasia grisea* 130mm

A dark-coloured tree skink from closed canopy forests. Body slender; paravertebrals not widened; ventrals 57–69; midbody scale rows 26–30; lamellae under toe IV 16–19; three strong keels on dorsal scales; prefrontals in broad contact; supranasals in broad contact; dorsum light or dark brown with 8–14 narrow dark rings; dark-banded tail; the banded pattern is more distinct in the young, becoming obscure with growth; and venter bright green. Inhabits lowland dipterocarp forests, 2–5m up on tree trunks, and feeds on ants, termites, beetles, snails, as well as fruits; clutches of 2–6 eggs, measuring 22.5–24.0 x 14.5–15.5mm, are produced at a time, and hatchlings are 46–52mm. This forest skink is known from Sarawak, Sabah and Kalimantan, its distribution encompassing the Malay Peninsula, Borneo, Sumatra and the Philippines.

Olive Tree Skink *Dasia olivacea* 115mm

A familiar tree skink, this species inhabits open forests. Body robust; scales under the tail not large; ear-opening small; paravertebrals not widened; ventrals 45–59; midbody scale rows 28–30; between 3–5 weak keels on dorsal scales; midbody scale rows 28–30; vertebrals 41–46; lamellae under toe IV 17–21; postorbital bone present; two large heel scales in males; dorsum olive to greenish-brown, sometimes black-spotted; venter unpatterned green; juvenile dorsum golden-yellow, with 13–16 dark transverse bands, each three scales wide, broader than the orange-yellow bands. Inhabits forests in the lowlands, up to 1,200m; utilises tree trunks and branches, ascending to the level of the canopy, and associated with large trees, especially at the edges of clearings, sheltering under peeling bark. Diet comprises bees, beetles, ants and flies, and other arthropods. 6–14 eggs, measuring 18.0–19.5 x 10.0–12.0mm, are produced, with more than a single clutch possible in the year; hatchlings measure 32–38mm. Known from Sarawak, Sabah and Kalimantan, it is widespread from Myanmar, Thailand, Cambodia, the Malay Peninsula, to Sumatra, Borneo, Java, Natuna and the Nicobar Archipelagos.

Mangrove Skink *Emoia atrocostata* 97.5mm

A common sandy and rocky beach and mangrove forest lizard. Body slender; limbs and tail well-developed; snout tapered; prefrontals narrowly in contact to separated; inter-parietal distinct, narrow; auricular lobules present; supralabials 6–8; infralabials 6–7; lamellae under toe IV 30–42; dorsum greyish-olive, flecked with dark brownish-grey; and venter bluish-grey to cream, with dark pigmentation under the throat. Inhabits coastal regions, including both sandy and rocky beaches, sheltering inside hollow tree trunks during high tide. Diurnal. Diet comprises small crabs, termites, fishes and other lizards; and 1–3 eggs, measuring 8 x 20mm, are produced at a time. Eggs are deposited inside piles of driftwood and tree-holes. Recorded from Brunei, Sarawak, Sabah and Kalimantan, it is a widespread species, known from Malay Peninsula, Sumatra, Borneo, Java, east to New Guinea, the Solomon Islands and northern Australia

Blue-tailed Skink *Emoia caeruleocauda* 50.9mm

A seashore-dwelling lizard with a blue tail. Body robust; snout short, tapering; frontonasal broader than long, in contact with rostral and with frontal; parietal in contact with interparietal; interparietal distinct; one pair of large nuchals; supraoculars four; supralabials eight, the last reduced in size; tympanum smaller than eye, with three anterior auricular lobules; midbody scale rows 16, smooth; supraoculars four; dorsal surface of body with a dark vertebral stripe in males, yellow in females, and undersurface of tail blue. Inhabits sandy beaches of offshore islands. Diurnal and terrestrial. Two eggs are produced at a time and hatchlings measure 22.4mm. This beautiful skink is known from islands to the east of Sabah; and also, Sulawesi, New Guinea, east to Fiji and the Solomon Islands.

Vyner's Tree Skink *Lamprolepis vyneri* 66mm

A rare, arboreal skink, only known from a few localities from the low hills of central Sarawak, Sabah and Kalimantan. Body slender; snout obtusely pointed; lower eyelid scaly; supranasals present, failing to contact each other; frontonasal as broad as long, in contact with rostral, but not with frontal; supraoculars five; supraciliaries eight; one pair of nuchals; tympanum small; midbody scale rows 21–22; preanals slightly larger than preceding scales; body scales smooth; lamellae under toe IV 20; tail relatively short, equal in length to those of head and body; head olive-grey, some scales edged with black; dorsal surface of body with four longitudinal stripes, consisting of a series of black dorsal scales that show a central olive-grey area; flanks of body and neck with black-edged brown scales; tail greyish-olive; and venter pale green. Inhabits low hills of Borneo; nothing is known of its diet or reproductive habits. This lizard is endemic to Borneo.

Bornean Striped Skink
Lipinia inexpectata 40.6mm

A skink species from lowland sites in Sabah, Sarawak and Kalimantan. Body slender; snout acute; external ear-opening absent; lower eyelid with a clear spectacle; midbody scale rows 20; longitudinal scale rows between parietals and base of tail 46–50; lamellae under toe IV 16–17; supralabials six; infralabials 6–7; subcaudals 68–74; dorsum tan-brown with a series of dark grey-brown stripes; paired paravertebral stripes from behind eye to tail-tip; paired dorsal stripes from temporals to inguinal region. Known from isolated lowland localities in Borneo, and have been found under rotting logs. The diet of this species is unknown. Two eggs are produced at a time. Endemic to Borneo.

Sarawak Striped Skink *Lipinia nitens* 33.6mm

A poorly-known, terrestrial skink, known only from Gunung Pueh and Gunung Matang, in western Sarawak. Body slender; snout pointed; two enlarged paravertebral scale rows; dorsal and lateral scales smooth; external ear-opening absent; limbs reduced, scarcely meeting when adpressed; midbody scale rows 20–22; lamellae under toe IV 16; supralabials six, supralabial four in suborbital position; median preanal scales large; subcaudal scales enlarged; dorsal surface metallic-green; sides of body spotted with black and green; pale yellow vertebral stripe, with jagged-edged black lines, one on each side from supraorbital to tail-base. Inhabits lowland forests and diet includes ants. Its reproductive habits remain unknown. Known from two isolated localities in western Borneo.

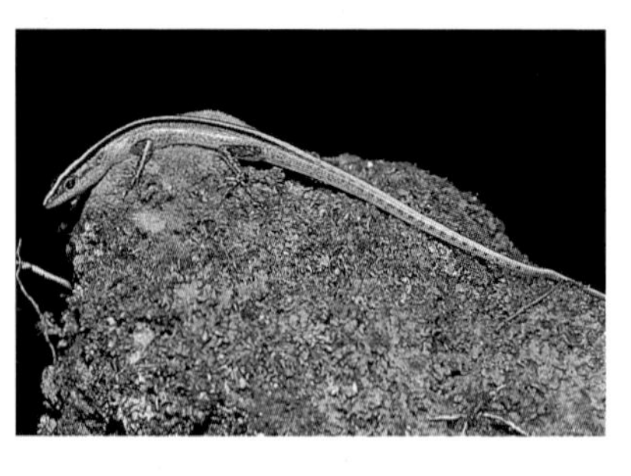

Common Striped Skink *Lipinia vittigera* 42mm

A common arboreal skink from lowland forests. Body slender; tail long, slender, tapering; snout elongate and acute; lower eyelid with transparent disc; ear-opening small; midbody scale rows 28, smooth; toe IV lamellae 25; dorsum brownish-black, with a bright yellow vertebral stripe, commencing from snout-tip; flanks with dark and pale spots. Inhabits lowland forests, and active on tree trunks and buttresses, while sheltering under exfoliating tree barks. Diet comprises small insects. Clutches of 2–4 eggs are laid at a time. Known from Sarawak and Sabah, it is distributed from southern Myanmar, Thailand, Laos, the Malay Peninsula, to the Mentawai Archipelago, Sumatra and Borneo.

Supple Skink *Lygosoma bowringii* 58mm

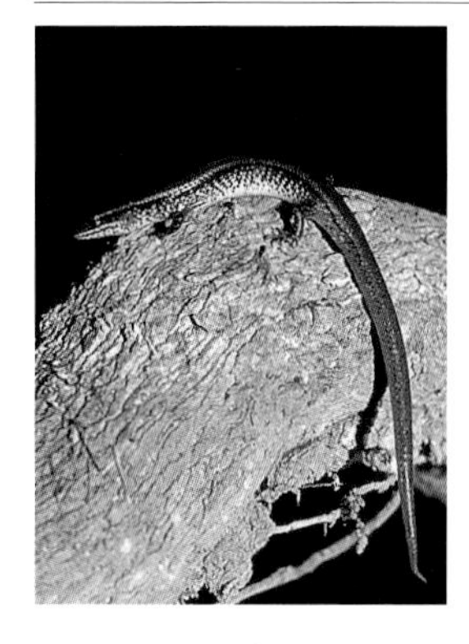

A common, garden skink, frequently seen in urban areas. Body slender, elongate; head scarcely distinct from neck; lower eyelid scaly; ear-opening small, rounded, lacking lobules; limbs reduced; scales smooth or weakly keeled; supranasals large; supralabials 6–7; infralabials 6–7; midbody scale rows 24–28; vertebrals 52–62; lamellae under toe IV 10–13; dorsum bronze-brown; a yellow stripe from back of head to tail; a black stripe below it also up to tail; paravertebral stripe golden-yellow, lateral stripe black; scales on flanks cream with black edges; venter yellow in males during the breeding season; tails of juveniles bright red, becoming grey or brown with age. More abundant in disturbed areas than in forests; its diet comprises small insects. Clutches comprising 2–4 eggs, measuring 7.3 x 12.4mm, are produced at a time. Hatchlings measure 22–23mm. A familiar, widespread species, known from Brunei, Sarawak and Sabah, but not from Kalimantan, it ranges from Myanmar, Andaman Islands, Thailand, the Malay Peninsula, to Borneo, Java, Sulawesi, possibly Sumatra, Vietnam, Cambodia, Laos and the Sulu Archipelago of the southern Philippines. It has been introduced onto Christmas Island in the Indian Ocean.

Common Sun Skink *Eutropis multifasciata* 137mm

A familiar terrestrial skink, widespread in Borneo. Body robust; lower eyelid scaly; dorsal scales with three, rarely five, keels; supralabials 6–7; infralabials 6–7; midbody scale rows 30–35; vertebrals 42–48; lamellae under toe IV 16–20; dorsum bronze-brown, with an orange or reddish-orange lateral band; venter unpatterned cream. Inhabits disturbed habitats, including forest clearings, it is active by day. Diet comprises primarily of arthropods, including cockroaches, isopods and spiders; smaller lizards may also be consumed occasionally. Ovoviviparous, giving birth to 1–10 live young, measuring 33.1–43.0mm. Found throughout Borneo (Brunei, Sarawak, Sabah and Kalimantan), from sea level to 1,800m, the distribution extends from southern China and north-eastern India, through Indo-China and the Malay Peninsula to the Greater and Lesser Sundas and Philippines. Records from New Guinea may be through human introductions.

Black-banded Skink *Eutropis rudis* 120mm

A small terrestrial forest skink, with a rough forehead. Body robust; forehead scales at posterior rugose; dorsal scales with three strong keels; supraciliaries six; supralabials 6–7; infralabials 6–7; midbody scale rows 28–30; lamellae under toe IV 18–21; dorsum olive-brown, with a light-edged dark brown line on the side; throat of adult males crimson, sometimes dark-spotted; that of females, unpatterned cream; venter greenish-white. Inhabits forests in the lowlands and midhills up to an elevation of about 1,300m and active on the leaf litter. Diet includes grasshoppers, cockroaches, moths, flies and isopods; and clutches of 2–4 eggs laid. Known from Brunei, Sarawak, Sabah and Kalimantan, its range includes Sumatra, Mentawai Archipelago, Borneo, Nicobar Islands, the Sula Archipelago, Sulawesi and the Sulu Archipelago.

Red-throated Skink *Eutropis rugifera* 65mm

A semi-arboreal skink from the lowlands. Body robust; dorsal scales with five, rarely seven, distinct keels; lower eyelids scaly; ear-opening reduced, edged with lobules; supranasals narrow and widely separated; frontonasal wider than long, contacting rostral and frontal; prefrontals separate; supraciliaries 5–6; supralabials nine; infralabials seven; midbody scale rows 24–28; lamellae under toe IV 18–26; dorsum blackish-brown, with 5–7 greenish-cream longitudinal stripes, sometimes broken up to form spots; venter greenish-cream, and throat dark spotted; throat bright red in adults during the breeding season. Inhabits forests in the midhills and known to climb tree trunks up to about 2m. Diet comprises insects. Reproductive habits unknown. Within Borneo, it is known from Brunei, Sarawak and Sabah, its distribution extending from southern Thailand, Nicobar Islands, the Malay Peninsula, to Sumatra, Borneo, Java and Bali.

Slender Litter Skink *Sphenomorphus aesculeticola* 42mm

A small terrestrial/fossorial skink with reduced limbs. Body slender; head not wider than neck or trunk; limbs relatively short; prefrontals separated; supraoculars four; frontonasal absent; supraciliaries 8–10; midbody scale rows 28–30; lamellae under toe IV 6–10; dorsum brown, with many scales dark-spotted, forming a series of dark lines or chequered pattern; a dark lateral band; venter unpatterned cream. Inhabits oak-forest clad montane regions of northern Borneo, at elevations of 1,350-1,650m, and is a semi-fossorial species, hiding under rocks and logs. Diet presumably comprises small insects and their larvae. Two eggs are produced at a time. Hatchlings measure 15mm. This skink is known only from Gunung Kinabalu and adjacent mountains, in Sabah.

Blue-throated Litter Skink *Sphenomorphus cyanolaemus* 60mm

A blue-throated ground skink that can also climb trees. Body slender; limbs relatively long; ear-opening lacking lobules; prefrontals in broad contact with each other; anterior loreals two, superimposed; nuchals absent; supraoculars six; supraciliaries 12–15; supralabials 6–8; infralabials six; mental as wide as rostral; midbody scale rows 37–42, smooth; lamellae under toe IV 16–19; two large preanals; dorsum bronze- or olive-brown, with two rows of dark spots; dark dorsolateral stripe. Inhabits lowland forests, this species is diurnal and terrestrial/semi-arboreal, and capable of climbing trees up to at least 5m, to bask and avoid predation, and possibly also to forage. At night, they sleep on leaves of saplings overhanging hill streams, 30–50cm above water. Diet presumably comprises insects; two eggs, measuring 6 x 11mm, are deposited in ant heaps, within buttresses of trees. Hatchlings measure 25–26mm. Within Borneo, it is known from Brunei, Sarawak and Sabah; extra-Bornean populations have been recorded from the Malay Peninsula and Sumatra.

Haas' Litter Skink *Sphenomorphus haasi* 57mm

A small terrestrial skink from western Sarawak. Body slender; ear-opening lacking lobules; tail thick basally, tapering to a point; snout obtuse; midbody scale rows 41–42, smooth; lamellae under toe IV 16–18; dorsum greyish-brown, with pale olive blotches, pale blue sclera of eye; dark dorsolateral band absent. Inhabits lowland forests of north-western Borneo, its diet presumably comprises small arthropods, and the species is generally active in the shade on tree buttresses and rocks during the day. The large eyes are suggestive of crepuscular habits and/or activity in areas of low light. Reproductive habits remain unstudied, although this is an oviparous species. Restricted to Sarawak and Sabah, and an endemic of Borneo.

Kinabalu Litter Skink *Sphenomorphus kinabaluensis* 58mm

A montane skink found commonly in Gunung Kinabalu and the Crocker Range of Sabah. Body slender; limbs long; prefrontals in wide contact with each other; supraculars five; parietals not in contact with supraoculars; supralabials seven; infralabials seven; nuchals absent; midbody scale rows 32–38; lamellae under toe IV 15–17; tail thick; dorsum light to dark brown, with several longitudinal rows of dark brown to yellow spots and occasionally also, dark brown speckles; a black dorsolateral stripe with small yellowish flecks. Inhabits altitudes between 1,600–2,200m; its diet comprises insects. Between 1–2 eggs, measuring 9.8–13.8 x 7.9–9.4mm, are produced, nests sometimes sited within ant nests, in tunnels in fallen trees of moss forests. Hatchlings measure 20.1– 21.5mm. This species is restricted to northern Borneo.

Many-scaled Litter Skink *Sphenomorphus multisquamatus*
68.5mm

A large, terrestrial skink, widespread in western and northern Borneo. Body robust; snout very short; body longer than tail; auricular lobules lacking; prefrontals in broad contact; nuchals absent; supraoculars 6–7; supraciliaries 14–15; supralabials 6–7; infralabials five; midbody scale rows 40–49; lamellae under toe IV 18–23; dorsum dark greyish-brown, with 2–4 rows of squarish black spots, with or without dark dorsolateral bands; and bright yellow ring around the eye. Inhabits lowland rainforests and peat swamps, its diet comprises small insects. Nothing is known of its reproductive biology. This species is known from Sarawak and Sabah, and is an endemic of Borneo.

Gunung Murud Litter Skink *Sphenomorphus murudensis*
49.3mm

A montane skink from the Gunung Murud massif in Sarawak. Body slender; snout rounded; lower eyelid scaly; ear lobules absent; supranasals absent; nostrils in a single nasal; prefrontals in contact; supraoculars six; parietals in contact with supraoculars; supraciliaries eight; supralabials six, the fourth in mid-orbital position; midbody scale rows 30–32, scales smooth; ventrals larger than dorsals; preanals enlarged; toe IV lamellae 16; dorsum dark brown, with black spots; a dark band on the sides; and hatchlings and juveniles with reddish-brown tails. Inhabits summits at altitudes of 1,500–2,400m. Diet remains unknown. Two eggs, measuring 17.3 x 10.5 and 18.0 x 10.7mm, are deposited in deep crevices in the soil. Endemic to Gunung Murud, in north-western Borneo.

Sabah Litter Skink *Sphenomorphus sabanus* 58mm

A litter skink widespread in Sabah, with two isolated records from east and west Kalimantan. Body robust; lobules in ear-opening absent; prefrontals in broad contact or separated; parietals in contact with supraoculars; supraoculars usually six; supraciliaries 14–17; supralabials seven; infralabials 5–7; midbody scale rows 38–42; lamellae under toe IV 18–22; dorsal surface brown to greyish-brown, with indistinct light spots, lacking dark dorsolateral bands; sides of neck and flanks of males ringed with orange; lips barred with black; males usually with an orange flush on flanks; and venter unpatterned cream. The distribution of this skink ranges from lowlands to submontane forests, and it is often associated with tree trunks and buttresses, and is a shade-loving lizard. Known to hang upside-down on a branch, suspended by its hind limbs, a behaviour considered mimicry of a dry twig. Its diet consists of beetles and spiders, although ants, cockroaches, grasshoppers, moths and flies are also consumed. Eggs, between 2–3 in number, measuring 10–12mm in length, are produced at a time.

Beccari's Water Skink *Tropidophorus beccarii* 98mm

A smooth-scaled water skink from the low hills of Borneo. Body robust in adults, slender in juveniles; scales smooth at least in adults; forehead scales smooth; prefrontals in broad contact or separated; tympanum smaller than orbit of eye; supraoculars 4–5; supraciliaries 6–7; supralabials 7–8; infralabials 4–5; midbody scale rows 28–30; lamellae under toe IV 19–21; dorsum dark brown or reddish-brown, with dark brown blotches and cross-bars; sides of head and flanks with light spots; a broad dark stripe extends on flanks, where they have vertical light bars or wedge-shaped marks. Inhabits rocky streams within dipterocarp forests, up to about 1,000m. Diet comprises water insects. Ovoviviparous, giving birth to four live young, measuring 30mm. Bornean records are from Brunei, Sarawak, Sabah and Kalimantan. This species is endemic to Borneo.

Brookes' Water Skink *Tropidophorus brookei* 101mm

The commonest Bornean water skink; body robust in adults, slender in juveniles; tympanum smaller than orbit of eye; supraciliaries 14; supraoculars five; supralabials eight; infralabials five; a single postmental; midbody scale rows 32, keeled, forming eight longitudinal lines on dorsum and oblique ones on flanks; dorsum dark brown with darker spots and blotches that may form transverse bands; a black spot on sides of neck; flanks with dark and white spots. Inhabits rocky streams in lowland dipterocarp forests. Diurnal and semi-aquatic, they are known from non-riparian portions of the forest, from small rocky hill streams. Juveniles and adult females are found sleeping on leaves and stems of saplings overhanging hill streams, clefts in rock faces of waterfalls and buttresses, 15–225cm above substrate. Adult males sleep inside rocky clefts within and along streams. Diet presumably aquatic arthropods. Ovoviviparous, between 1–5 young are produced at a time. This lizard is endemic to Borneo, with records from Brunei, Sarawak, Sabah and Kalimantan.

Small-legged Water Skink *Tropidophorus micropus* 40mm

A poorly-known water skink from central and northern Borneo. Body slender; scales on forehead distinctly striated; frontonasal as long as broad; supraoculars four; supraciliaries seven; scales on flanks relatively small; ventrals smooth, larger than laterals; midbody scale rows 34; subdigital lamellae smooth; dorsum dark brown, with a black spot on sides of neck; and venter cream, with irregular dark spots. Inhabits rocky streams within lowland forests. Retreat sites include fallen tree trunks and cracks in rocks, including under waterfalls. When molested, the species excretes an unpleasant-smelling musk from the cloacal glands. Diet remains unknown, and likely to be aquatic arthropods. Ovoviviparous, three young ones are produced at a time, measuring 26.0–27.4mm. This species is endemic to Borneo, with records from Sarawak, Sabah and Kalimantan.

Mocquard's Water Skink *Tropidophorus mocquardii* 95mm

A high-elevation water skink, from northern Borneo. Body slender; forehead scales smooth; tympanum smaller than orbit of eye; supraoculars five; supralabials seven; infralabials five; midbody scale rows 34, smooth at least in adults; digits short with smooth lamellae; dorsum brown, with dark transverse bands; flanks with white spots; and venter cream. Inhabits the midhills of Gunung Kinabalu, in Sabah. Its diet and reproductive habits remain unstudied. This species is endemic to northern Borneo.

VARANIDAE (MONITOR LIZARDS)

Monitors are the largest of the living lizards. They are swift and active predators of small mammals, birds, bird eggs, reptiles, amphibians, as well as invertebrates. Their forked tongue that is flicked in and out, to taste the chemical nature of the environment, is reminiscent of snakes. The Water Monitor is one of three largest lizards in the world, and is known to congregate on turtle nesting beaches to eat eggs and hatchlings. They are day-active, and forage on land, as well as in water, and some species frequently climb trees in search of bird eggs and nestlings.

Dumeril's Monitor
Varanus dumerilii 1.5m

A brightly-coloured monitor from lowlands, especially mangrove swamps. Body short, robust, head small, flattened; snout short and broad; nostrils elongated; tympanum large, rounded; nuchal scales oval, flat, smooth or posteriorly feebly keeled; abdominal scales weakly keeled, in 37–41 rows; tail laterally compressed; forehead orange or yellowish-orange, especially in juveniles, becoming tan or yellow with growth; dorsum brownish-yellow or tan, with a dark temporal streak from eye to ear; dark vertical bars on lips; throat yellow with 6–8 orange stripes; venter yellow with dark transverse bars. Associated with lowland forests and the midhills, especially in mangrove swamps. Semi-aquatic and capable of both burrowing and swimming, and apparently specializing in crabs, although invertebrates, including ants, scorpions, beetle larvae, spiders, fishes, other lizards, eggs and rodents are also consumed. Clutches of 12–16, more rarely up to 23, are produced, that hatch after 215–234 days; hatchlings are 81–83.5mm. This beautiful monitor is known from southern Myanmar, Thailand, the Malay Peninsula, Sumatra, Borneo (Brunei, Sarawak, Sabah and Kalimantan), Pulau Bangka and Pulau Belitung.

Rough-necked Monitor *Varanus rudicollis* 1.46m

A dark, rough-necked tree monitor, widespread in the lowlands. Body slender; snout relatively long; nuchal scales strongly keeled; abdominal scales keeled, in 79–90 transverse rows; body and neck somewhat slender; limbs relatively thin; dorsum almost black in adults, with yellow tinge on neck and foreparts of body in juveniles; neck with three black stripes; flanks with yellow ocelli; hatchlings with yellow and black horizontal bands on venter of body. Inhabits lowland forests, its diet comprises ants, termites, stick insects, cockroaches, grasshoppers, spiders, scorpions, and also, small mammals, frogs, fishes and crabs. Between 13–14 eggs are produced, and up to three clutches are known a year. Incubation period is 180–184 days, hatchlings measuring 23.8–26.0cm. Within Borneo, it is known from Sarawak, Sabah and Kalimantan, its range extending from southern Myanmar, Thailand, the Malay Peninsula, Sumatra, Pulau Bangka and Borneo.

Water Monitor *Varanus salvator* 3m

A large monitor, commonly seen near waterbodies. Body robust in adults, slender in juveniles; snout depressed; nostril rounded or oval, twice as far from orbit as from snout tip; nuchal scale strongly keeled; crown scales large, flat, smooth, larger than nuchal scales; supraoculars well differentiated; midventral scales feebly keeled, numbering 148–153; tail strongly compressed with a double-toothed crest above; caudal scales keeled dorsally and ventrally; juveniles dark dorsally, yellow-spotted or ocelli in transverse series; snout black-barred, especially on lips; venter yellow with narrow, and black vertical V-shaped marks extending to sides of venter; dorsum darkens with growth, and occasionally, all vestiges of yellow chain-like pattern are lost. Inhabits a variety of habitats, ranging from mangrove swamps, river banks, canals, to dipterocarp forests, and is frequently seen in urban settings. Diet comprises a wide variety of large invertebrates and small vertebrates, such as insects, fishes, crabs, freshwater turtles, eggs as well as adults of water birds, crocodiles and sea turtles, other varanids and rodents, including carrion. Between 5–30 eggs, measuring 32.3–42.9 x 64.0–82.6mm, are produced. Incubation period is 180–327 days, depending on locality, and hatchlings measure 18.0–30.0cm. Known from Brunei, Sarawak, Sabah and Kalimantan, this lizard is widespread, from Sri Lanka and India, southern China, through South-east Asia, to the Lesser Sundas and the Philippines. This species is hunted for its skin and for meat throughout its range (more than 1 million skins per annum), but perhaps as a result of its adaptability to altered habitats, remains common, even abundant, in many localities.

CROCODYLIDAE (CROCODILES)

Crocodiles are distinctive, with their heavy jaws and heavily armoured bodies. Three species of crocodilian occur on Borneo, one from saltwater habitats, two from freshwaters. They are predators of small to large-sized prey, and some large-growing individuals may pose danger to humans and livestock. All species are linked to wetlands, such as rivers, lakes, dams and mangroves. They lay eggs and the sex of all crocodiles is determined by the incubation temperature of these eggs.

Saltwater Crocodile *Crocodylus porosus* 6.2m

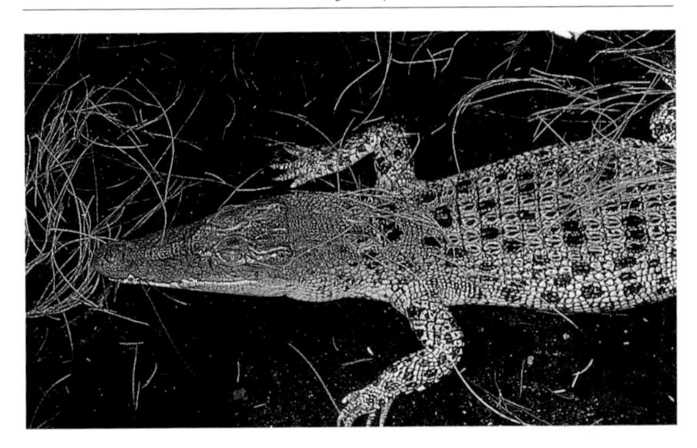

A large head and a heavy snout, with a pair of ridges running from orbit to the centre of snout; scales on back are more oval than in most other crocodiles. Juveniles more brightly coloured than adults, being black-spotted or blotched on a pale yellow or grey background. Inhabits rivers and coasts, especially areas with mangrove forests, and generally in areas with tidal influence, and more rarely, in standing bodies of water. Juveniles feed on crabs, shrimps, insects, fish, lizards and snakes; adults can take turtles, birds and mammals. Large-growing crocodiles of this species are occasionally known to attack humans, and in Sarawak, several rivers, including the Batang Lupar, have acquired notoriety for cases of crocodile predation on humans. A mound-nest is constructed by the female crocodile, in which 60–80 eggs are deposited. Females guard the nest till the eggs hatch, transporting the young ones to the water. Distributed from India, Sri Lanka, through Indo-Malaya, to New Guinea, the Philippines, Australia and islands in South Pacific, in estuaries, as well as in rivers and lakes.

Malayan False Gharial *Tomistoma schlegelii* 5.5m
A narrow-snouted species that eats mostly fish, although other small animals, including monkeys, are also reportedly eaten. Dorsum is brown with black spots and bands, the tail with broad black bands. Juveniles are bright yellow, also with dark bands. Unlike in crocodiles, the iris of the false gharial is distinctly yellowish-brown. Inhabits freshwaters, like rivers, swamps and lakes overgrown with vegetation. It makes a mound nest on peat or a mixture of peat and humus, within or close to roots of large trees, about 60cm high, located adjacent to water. In here, 20–60 elliptical eggs are laid that hatch in 75–90 days. Threatened due to habitat disturbance, including the transformation of low-lying areas for agriculture; fragmentation of habitat as a result of logging; and perhaps also hunting for its skin. A Sundaic species, restricted to the Malay Peninsula, Sumatra, Borneo (Sarawak and Kalimantan), Java, and possibly Sulawesi. However, populations on mainland Asia are relictual, and viable groups survive only on Sumatra and western Borneo.

BATAGURIDAE (ASIAN HARDSHELLED TURTLES)

These are hardshelled turtles that are primarily aquatic, although a few are terrestrial, showing large scales on their limbs as well as a 'high walk', like tortoises. The shell bears scutes and the snout lacks the pig-like tubular structure seen in softshelled turtles. There is a general tendency towards herbivory, although some are specialized feeders of fish and crustaceans, and a few show enlarged heads and associated jaw muscles for tackling hard-bodied prey such as molluscs. Eggs are hardshelled, elongated, and buried along banks of water bodies.

Painted Terrapin *Callagur borneoensis* 41cm

A very large (about 41cm in adult females; 39cm in adult males) hardshelled turtle, recognisable from relatives in possessing a flattened carapace, which is light brown or olive, with three black longitudinal stripes. In juveniles, the shell is flattened, and the vertebral keel distinct. The head of females is olive, while non-breeding males have grey heads. During the breeding season, the heads of adult males turn white, and a red stripe develops on the forehead, between the eyes. Males also have relatively longer and thicker tails that project out of the rim of the carapace. Only aquatic plants are eaten by this turtle. A nesting migration occurs, adults travelling as far as 3km downriver, to nest on sea beaches, along with sea turtles. Eggs are elongated, measuring 68–76 x 36–44mm, and clutch size is about 12, eggs taking 69–82 days to hatch. The species inhabits the tidal portions of rivers, and may occur in estuaries, from southern Thailand, through Peninsular Malaysia, to Sumatra and Borneo (Sarawak and Kalimantan).

Malayan Box Turtle *Cuora amboinensis* 216mm

Unique among turtles of Borneo in possessing a well-developed hinge on plastron that allows shell to be completely closed, with head and limbs tucked in, this turtle is unmistakable. Shell high-domed and smooth; a single keel in the centre of carapace in adults; juveniles with two additional keels laterally; carapace olive, brown or nearly black, plastron yellow or cream, with a single black blotch; face with yellow longitudinal stripes. Adult males show a concavity in plastra, while adult females have flat plastra. It inhabits both standing and slow-flowing water bodies, including rivers, lakes, marshes, mangrove swamps, as well as agricultural areas; juveniles are more aquatic than almost exclusively aquatic adults. Largely herbivorous, it feeds on water plants and fungi, although worms and aquatic insects are also consumed. Eggs are elongated, and clutch size is 1–6, two clutches being laid a year. Eggs measure 40–55 x 25–34mm and hatch 1.5–3 months later. Reported from Brunei, Sarawak, Sabah and Kalimantan, its distribution is wide in tropical regions of South-east Asia, from north-eastern India through Bangladesh, Myanmar, Thailand, Indo-China, the Malay Peninsula, to Borneo, Sumatra, Java, and smaller islands to east, in addition to islands of the Philippines.

Asian Leaf Turtle *Cyclemys dentata* 240mm

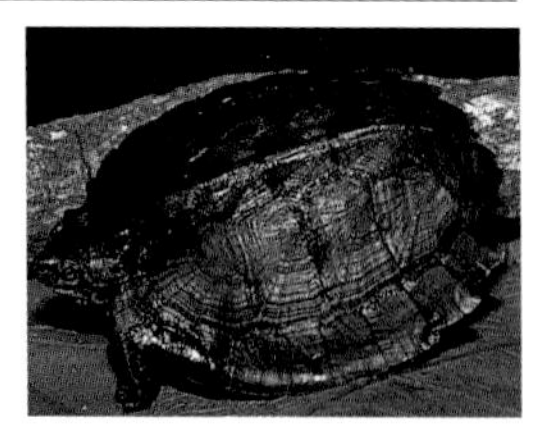

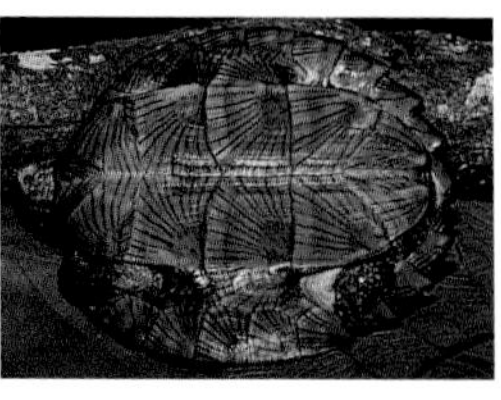

An extremely variable species, with an oval, depressed shell that bears three keels and large scales on back of head; plastron with a hinge in adult turtles around 23–25cm in shell length. Both carapace and plastron are brown, sometimes with dark radiating lines. Females are the larger of the sexes, and possess relatively shorter tails than males, which fail to project out of the carapace rim. Found in both highlands and plains, although more common at lower elevations, this turtle occurs in small rivers, streams, as well as in ponds. Juveniles are more aquatic than adults, the latter more of a bottom-walker than a true swimmer. It is thought that the leaf-like shape and colour of the shell aids the turtle in taking shelter on the forest floor. Like many land tortoises, this turtle defaecates when picked up. Both plants and animals are eaten, and leaf turtles are known to feast on figs. Nests are dug in ground, where 2–4 elongated hard-shelled eggs are laid. These hatch nearly two and half months later. Known from Brunei, Sarawak, Sabah and Kalimantan, its distribution includes the Malay Peninsula, Sumatra, Java, Borneo and the Philippines.

Spiny Turtle *Heosemys spinosa* 220mm

The young ones of this turtle resemble pin-cushions, with greatly expanded marginals, bearing distinct spines that disappear or become less obvious with growth, or through wear and tear. It is thought that these spines act as a deterrent to predators, such as snakes. Carapace oval, with a strong vertebral keel. There are dark radiating lines on pale brown plastron and under marginal scales; head brown, usually with a yellow spot behind eye; fingers and toes are partially-webbed; hind limbs club-shaped. Adult males possess relatively longer and thicker tails than adult females. This species inhabits forests, usually in the middle elevations, and may be found far from water. It feeds on both plants and animal matter. Three elongated, hard-shelled eggs are laid, and to enable passage of these relatively large eggs, a hinge develops in the plastron. Hatchlings measure 63mm. Known from Brunei, Sarawak, Sabah and Kalimantan, its distribution including southern Myanmar, Thailand, the Malay Peninsula, to Sumatra, Borneo and the Natunas.

Malayan Flat-shelled Turtle *Notochelys platynota* 320mm

This familiar turtle can be identifiable from its flat carapace that bears 6–7 vertebrals (all other freshwater turtles from Borneo show five vertebrals). It has a low, interrupted vertebral keel and its flattened carapace is olive, yellowish-brown or brick-red in colour, whilst hatchlings have a bright green carapace. Head brown, juveniles with two yellow longitudinal stripes; a weak hinge on plastron; toes fully webbed. Adult males, besides showing relatively longer and thicker tails, possess slightly concave plastra. Inhabits shallow water bodies, with an abundance of water plants, such as marshes, swamps and forest streams. It is an herbivore, feeding mostly on water plants. A 205mm female produces three large, hard-shelled eggs, measuring 56 x 27–28mm. Within Borneo, it is known from Brunei, Sarawak, Sabah and Kalimantan, its distribution encompassing southern Thailand, Vietnam, the Malay Peninsula, to Sumatra, Java and Borneo.

Malayan Giant Turtle *Orlitia borneensis* 800mm

A huge freshwater turtle from the large rivers and lakes of Peninsular Malaysia, Sumatra and Borneo. A narrow, unpatterned black, brown or grey carapace, the plastron being paler. Carapace humped in juveniles, turning smooth with growth; adults with a relatively narrower shell; head large, broad chewing surface suggestive of a primarily herbivorous diet; band-like scales on outer faces of forelimbs; fingers and toes extensively webbed; head dark, with a pale line from mouth to back of head. Adult males can be recognized in that they possess relatively longer and thicker tails. Little is known of the species' ecology and behaviour, except that eggs are elongated, with brittle hard shells, measuring on average 80 x 40mm. Hatchlings are about 60mm, with rough texture to their shells and markedly serrated marginals at carapace posterior. Although the wild diet is unknown, in captivity, this turtle accepts both plants and animal food, on land and in water. Known from isolated localities in Sarawak and Kalimantan, especially from large, peat swamp lakes.

Black Marsh Turtle *Siebenrockiella crassicollis* 200mm

A medium-sized black freshwater turtle, it can be distinguished from other Bornean turtles in showing three keels on juvenile carapaces (although adults have a single keel). Carapace also bears serrated posterior marginals, and vertebral region of adults flattened. Adult males have relatively longer and thicker tails, and slightly concave plastra; adult females retain light head-spots, while these markings fade with growth in males. Inhabits slow-moving or standing bodies of waters, such as marshes, ponds, streams and lakes. Most of its time is spent buried in the mud at the bottom of the water, and its carnivorous diet includes aquatic animals, such as worms, snails, shrimps and frogs, and it will also scavenge on dead animals. Although feeding takes place in water, it will also come on land at night to forage. Males court by bobbing their heads while pursuing them. 3–4 clutches of just 1–2 eggs, measuring 45 x 19mm, are laid. Hatchlings measure 52mm. Reported from Sarawak and Kalimantan, this species is distributed from southern Myanmar, south to Vietnam, Thailand, the Malay Peninsula, to Sumatra, Java and Borneo.

CHELONIIDAE (MARINE TURTLES)

All but one species of marine turtles belong to this family. They are exclusively marine in habits, and only the adult females come ashore (to lay eggs). Widespread in the warm seas of the world, marine turtles are threatened by a variety of human activities, from hunting for their flesh and shell scutes, to pollution of marine habitats and destruction of nesting beaches.

Green Turtle *Chelonia mydas* 1.4m

A large sea turtle, showing a pair of prefrontal scales on forehead; scutes of carapace not overlapping; upper jaw without a hook; forelimbs with a single claw; carapace olive or brown, usually with a dark radiating pattern; plastron pale yellow. The English name is for the colour of its fat, once in demand for making turtle soup. Adult males are smaller than females and possess relatively longer tails, which project out of carapace rim. Juveniles are carnivorous, while adults consume only sea grasses and seaweeds. Eggs are soft-shelled, spherical, each nest containing 98–172 eggs, measuring 41.4–42.1mm, hatching about 60 days later. Up to 11 nests may be laid by a female within a nesting season. Collection of eggs from nests, disturbance of nesting turtles, including their capture for food and destruction of nesting beaches globally threaten this species. As in most other turtles, incubation temperature of egg determines sex of hatchling. Nesting takes place on Bornean coasts and on small offshore islands, and this species is widely distributed in tropical regions, while particularly common around oceanic islands and along coasts with wide sandy beaches.

Hawksbill Sea Turtle *Eretmochelys imbricata* 1m

Slightly smaller than the Green Turtle, this is nonetheless a large sea turtle. Carapace heart-shaped; scutes of carapace with four pairs of imbricate costal scutes; two pairs of prefrontal scales; upper jaw relatively narrow, elongate; upper jaw forward-projecting, to form a bird-like beak; carapace olive-brown, juveniles with darker blotches. Associated with reefs, bays, estuaries and lagoons; diet includes sponges, algae, corals and shellfish. Clutch size 96–177; eggs measuring 30–35mm and taking 57–65 days to hatch. This is the bearer of 'tortoiseshell', used in the production of combs, jewellery and trinkets. Its flesh is occasionally known to be poisonous, possibly from the algae it consumes. Isolated records from Borneo, this species is globally widespread but almost nowhere abundant.

Olive Ridley Sea Turtle *Lepidochelys olivacea* 80cm

The smallest and lightest of sea turtles. Carapace broad, heart-shaped, posterior marginals serrated, with juxtaposed costal scutes; 5–9 pairs of costals; bridge with four inframarginals, each with a pore; adult shell smooth; hatchling shell tricarinate, the lateral and vertebral keels disappearing with growth; upper jaw hooked, lacking a ridge; carapace olive-green or greyish-olive; plastron greenish-yellow; juveniles grey-black dorsally; cream ventrally. Although largest nesting aggregations ('arribadas') are known from eastern India, where several hundred thousand turtles congregate to nest, populations on Borneo (at Brunei, and smaller ones in Sabah and Sarawak) are small. Clutches comprise 50–160 eggs, measuring 34–43mm; incubation period is 45–60 days. Hatchlings measure 37.9–49.9mm. Widely distributed in the Indo-Pacific area, and within Borneo, significant nesting takes place only on the coast of Brunei Darussalam.

DERMOCHELYIDAE (LEATHERBACK SEA TURTLE)

This family includes a single living species (there are several fossil relatives), the Leatherback Sea Turtle, which is the largest of the turtles, and one of the heaviest living reptiles. It frequently wanders into cold Arctic waters, presumably in search of food, which is primarily jellyfish.

Leatherback Sea Turtle *Dermochelys coriacea* 2.5m

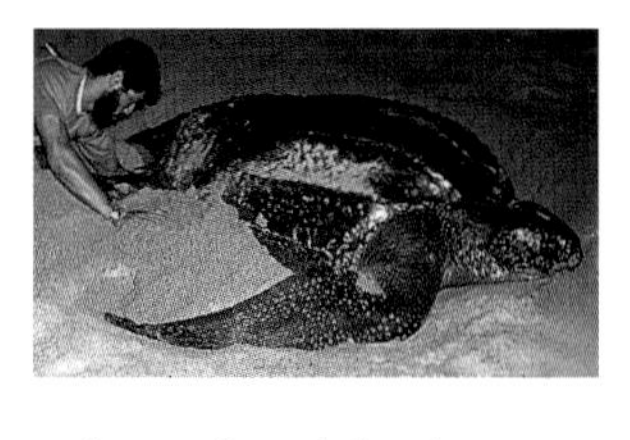

This is the largest of living turtles, as well as the largest and heaviest of living reptiles, known to attain a curved carapace length of over 256cm and weight of 916kg; shell is elongated, tapered towards end, bearing seven ridges on carapace and five on plastron; the entire shell is covered with skin in adults, although distinct scales or scale-like structures are present on hatchling shells; limbs are paddle-like and clawless. Feeds primarily on jellyfish, in northern temperate waters, and is capable of diving up to 1,200m below the surface in search of food. Nests are excavated on beaches that have uninterrupted open access from deep waters, and are deeper compared to other sea turtles. Clutches comprise 90–130 eggs, each spherical, soft-shelled, 50–54mm in diameter. Threatened because of capture for its fat (used in fixing leaks on wooden boats), collection of eggs and destruction of nesting habitats. Leatherbacks are known to eat plastic bags, apparently mistaking them for jellyfish. Widely distributed in both warm and cold seas, this is a turtle from the open ocean, visiting islands, such as Borneo, only to nest.

TESTUDINIDAE (LAND TORTOISES)

True tortoises are almost entirely herbivorous (although almost all will scavenge on carrion from time to time), recognisable in possessing columnar legs, rounded shells and heavy scales on limbs. They are adapted for a life on dry land, and many species can survive long periods without water. A single species occurs on Borneo, the Asian Giant Tortoise, which is fond of water, wallowing in forest streams for hours. Tortoises are known dispersal agents of forest plants.

Asian Giant Tortoise *Manouria emys* 500mm

The Asian Brown Tortoise is the largest of the land tortoises in Asia, weighing up to 20kg. Shell relatively low; vertebral region depressed; distinct growth rings on scutes of the carapace; upper jaw hooked; outer surface of forelimbs bear large scales; a pair of tuberculate scales on thighs; shell blackish-brown; plastron lighter. Largely herbivorous; insects and frogs are also eaten. It constructs a mound nest by sweeping leaf litter in which 23–51 hard-shelled, spherical eggs of diameter 51–54mm are deposited. Thereafter, it guards the nest, attacking egg predators. Incubation period is 60–75 days, and hatchlings are 60–66mm. Widespread in Borneo, but from isolated localities, and all from lowland and midhill, evergreen forests of eastern Sabah and southern Sarawak. The range of this species extends from north-eastern India, southern China, Indo-China and Indo-Malaya, and includes Sumatra, and two subspecies are recognised. This large tortoise is threatened by habitat destruction and hunting for food.

TRIONYCHIDAE (SOFTSHELLED TURTLES)

A skin-clad shell, just three claws on each limb and nostrils set on a fleshy proboscis immediately set these turtles apart from all others. Highly aquatic, they are found in rivers and ponds, and are primarily carnivorous, although water plants may also be consumed. Softshelled turtles are aggressive, and can deliver a painful bite, so even hatchlings need to be handled with caution.

Malayan Softshell Turtle *Amyda cartilaginea* 700mm

This is one of the commonest turtles, recognisable from its pig-like snout, skin-clad shell and rounded or oval carapace. The dorsal surface of the shell is greenish-grey or olive, sometimes with yellow-bordered black spots or radiating streaks, which tend to disappear with growth. Unlike the Asian Softshell Turtle *Dogania subplana*, this species has rounded (not straight) sides to its carapace and has a relatively narrow head. Over much of its range, they co-occur, appearing to replace it in lowlands, occurring in large muddy rivers, swamps and marshes. Adult males of both species have relatively longer tails that exceed carapace rim. In addition, in this turtle, plastron is white in males, grey in females. Inhabits wetlands at low elevations, and active at night, and carnivorous, feeding on fishes, frogs, shrimps and water insects. Nests of this turtle are holes on riverbanks, where 4–8 rounded eggs, measuring 21–33mm in diameter, are laid. These hatch in about four and a half months time. The species occurs in Brunei, Sarawak, Sabah and Kalimantan, its distribution extending from north-eastern India, Myanmar, Thailand, the Malay Peninsula, Vietnam to Sumatra, Java and Borneo.

Asian Softshell Turtle *Dogania subplana* 350mm

Top: adult; bottom: hatchling

A flat, oval, carapace with distinctly straight sides; head large, bearing a pig-like snout; carapace is covered with skin, and is dark olive or brown with a dark median stripe and 2–3 pairs of black-centred eye-like spots, a pattern most distinct in juveniles and fading with growth; plastron cream or grey. In juveniles, a reddish blotch occurs behind eyes, which disappears in adults. Adults develop a hinge on carapace that presumably allows them to hide under boulders along streams. A species from highlands, this turtle, inhabits clear rocky mountain streams. The large head of this turtle is thought to be adapted for cracking shells of molluscs, such as snails. Known from Brunei, Sarawak, Sabah and Kalimantan, its distribution extends from southern Myanmar to the Malay Peninsula, and also, Java, Sumatra, Borneo and some of the islands of the Philippines.

Asian Giant Softshell Turtle *Pelochelys cantorii* 1.5m

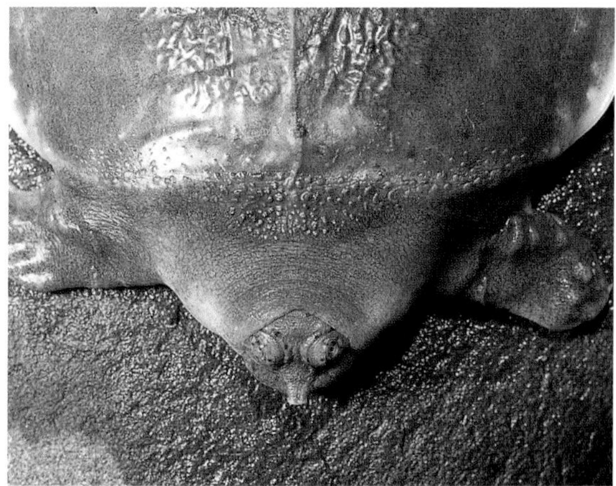

A large freshwater turtle. Shell low and depressed, elongated in young, oval in adults; juveniles with numerous tubercles on carapace and a low vertebral keel; proboscis extremely short and rounded; carapace olive or brown, spotted or streaked with lighter or darker shades, with a lighter outer edge. A coastal and riverine species, it feeds on fish, shrimps, crabs and molluscs, and sometimes also aquatic plants. Between 20–28 eggs are laid at a time. Bornean records are from Kampung Marak Parak, at the base of Kinabalu Park, besides southern and eastern Kalimantan. The global distribution of this turtle includes coastal Peninsular India, Bangladesh, Myanmar, Thailand, Peninsular Malaysia, Borneo, southern China and Vietnam.

Glossary

Adult Sexually mature individual.
Anterior Nearer the front (towards head).
Arboreal Species that live in trees or in other vegetation away from the ground.
Aquatic Species that live in water.
Canopy Layer of vegetation above ground, usually comprising tree branches and epiphytes.
Clutch Total number of eggs laid by a female at a time.
Clutch size Number of eggs in a nest.
Courtship Behaviour preceding mating.
Crepuscular Active during dawn and dusk.
Depressed Flattened from top to bottom.
Diurnal Active during day.
Dorsum Dorsal surface of body, excluding head and tail.
Endemic Restricted to a particular region.
Femoral pores Pores present on femoral region of some geckos.
Fossorial Species that live underground.
Infralabial Scales on lower lip.
Keel A narrow prominent ridge.
Lamella (pl. lamellae) Pads under digits in lizards (also scansor).
Litter Detritus of fallen leaves, branches and bark that accumulate on the forest floor.
Middorsal Scales around middle of body.
Nocturnal Active during night.
Oviparous Egg-laying.
Ovoviviparous Form of reproduction when the eggs develop within the body of the mother, who does not provide nutrition other than the yolk.
Posterior Nearer the back (towards tail).
Preanal pores Pores situated in front of cloaca in geckos.
Prefrontals Paired scales on anterior margin of orbit of eye, usually bounded by the frontal.
Recurved Curved or bent.
Reticulate Arranged like a net.
Scansor Pads under digits in geckos (also lamella).
Scute A horny epidermal shield.
Serrated Possessing a saw-toothed edge.
Subcaudal Scales below tail.
Supralabial Scales on upper lip.
Tubercle Knot-like projection.
Tympanum Ear-drum.
Vermiculation Pattern consisting of vague, worm-like markings.
Ventral Scales under body, from throat to vent.
Vertebral Pertaining to the region of the backbone.
Viviparous Live-bearing, whereby the embryo obtains additional nourishment from the mother, in addition to the yolk.

Further reading

Auliya, M. 2006. *Taxonomy, Life History and Conservation of Giant Reptiles in West Kalimantan (Indonesian Borneo).* Natur und Tier Verlag GmbH, Münster. 432 pp.

Auliya, M. 2007. *An Identification Guide to the Freshwater Turtles and Tortoises of Malaysia, Singapore, Indonesia, Brunei, the Philippines, East Timor and Papua New Guinea.* TRAFFIC South-east Asia, Kuala Lumpur. 98 pp.

Das, I. 1996. Lizards. In *Indonesian Heritage. Wildlife. Volume 5.* pp: 34–35. T. Whitten and J. Whitten (Eds.). Editions Didier Millet/Archipelago Press, Singapore.

Das, I. 2004. *A Pocket Guide. Lizards of Borneo.* Natural History Publications (Borneo) Sdn Bhd., Kota Kinabalu. 83 pp.

Das, I. 2010. *A Field Guide to the Reptiles of South-east Asia.* New Holland Publishers (UK), Ltd., London. 376 pp.

De Rooij, N. 1915. *The Reptiles of the Indo-Australian Archipelago. Vol. I.* Lacertilia, Chelonia, Emydosauria. E.J. Brill, Leiden. xiv + 384 pp.

Diong, C.H. 1998. Lizards. In *The Encyclopedia of Malaysia. Volume 3. Animals.* pp: 66–67. H.S. Yong (ed.). Archipelago Press, Singapore.

Inger, R.F. & F.L. Tan. 1996. *The Natural History of Amphibians and Reptiles in Sabah.* Natural History Publications (Borneo), Sdn. Bhd., Kota Kinabalu. vi + 101 pp.

Iskandar, D.T. 2000. *Turtles and Crocodiles of Insular Southeast Asia and New Guinea.* Institute of Technology, Bandung. xix + 191 pp. Bahasa Indonesia edition 2000: *Kura-kura & buaya Indonesia & Papua Nugini dengan catatan mengenai jenis–jenis di Asia Tenggara.* Institut Teknologi Bandung, Bandung. xix + 191 pp.

Lim, B.-L. & I. Das. 1999. *Turtles of Borneo and Peninsular Malaysia.* Natural History Publications (Borneo), Sdn. Bhd., Kota Kinabalu. xii + 151 pp.

Malkmus, R., U. Manthey, G. Vogel, P. Hoffmann & J. Kosuch. 2002. *Amphibians & Reptiles of Mount Kinabalu (North Borneo).* Koeltz Scientific Books, Königstein. 424 pp.

Manthey, U. & W. Grossmann. 1997. *Amphibien and Reptilien Südostasiens.* Natur und Tier Verlag, Münster. 512 pp.

Stuebing, R.B. & R.F. Inger. 1999. *A Field Guide to the Snakes of Borneo.* Natural History Publications (Borneo), Kota Kinabalu: v + 235 pp.

Tan, F.L. 1993. *Checklist of Lizards of Sabah.* Sabah Parks Trustees, Kota Kinabalu. (2) + 18 pp.

Index

Photographic Acknowledgements

Front cover: Sabah Pit Viper (*Popeia sabahi*).
Back cover: Blue-eyed Angle-headed Lizard (*Gonocephalus liogaster*).
Spine: Bornean Leaf-nosed Pit Viper (*Trimeresurus borneensis*)
Title page: Long-snouted Shrub Lizard (*Aphaniotis acutirostris*).

All photographs by Indraneil Das except:

Gernot Vogel: *18* (t).

Robert Inger: *25*, *37* (t), *44* (t).

Tan Heok Hui: *27* (t), *65*, *70* (t), *97* (t), *110* (b).

Ulrich Manthey: *1*, *33* (b), *42* (b), *71* (t), *73* (l, r), *77* (t), *105* (bl, br), *120* (b).

Norman Lim: *51* (t, b).

Jeet Sukumaran: *55*, *61* (t).

Robert Voeks: *62* (t).

Kelvin K.P. Lim: *35* (t).

Aaron Lobo: *67* (t), *69* (t).

Mark Auliya: *67* (b).

Björn Lardner: *85* (t, bl, br), *118* (t).

Chua Ee Kiam: *88*.

Showichi Sengoku: *104* (t).

Alain Compost: *107*.

John G. Frazier: *131*, *133* (b).